Other Spaces

This, the first account of the Royal Shakespeare Company's two small-scale theatres, The Other Place and The Warehouse, examines the exciting challenge offered to 'mainstream' drama by the fringe. Colin Chambers looks at the movement in the 1960s towards 'other spaces' — theatres made out of basements, halls, huts, and rooms. He shows how it came together with the experimental traditions of the RSC, at first in the figure of Buzz Goodbody, who started The Other Place and opened the way for that theatre's distinctive mix of the classical and the contemporary. Later came The Warehouse, with its commitment to new writing. The story of just how and why a major national and international company such as the RSC should run two little theatres like these includes problems and internal conflicts as well as notable public successes. The difficulties are analyzed alongside the string of achievements, from Buzz Goodbody's *Hamlet*, Trevor Nunn's *Macbeth,* and John Barton's *Merchant of Venice* to Brecht and contemporary work as diverse as David Edgar's *Destiny, Piaf* by Pam Gems, Edward Bond's *The Bundle*, and *Sons of Light* by David Rudkin. *Other Spaces* is an important historical record, with continuing relevance for the theatre of the 1980s.

A METHUEN THEATREFILE
in series with

The Plays of Edward Bond, by Tony Coult

The casebound edition of this book
forms part of the
THEATRE STUDIES
series from TQ Publications
which also includes

Beckett: a Theatre Bibliography, compiled by Virginia Cooke
Letters from a Theatrical Scene Painter, by T. W. Erle (1880)
A World Guide to Performing Arts Periodicals,
compiled by Christopher Edwards

Other Spaces
New Theatre and the RSC

Colin Chambers

London
EYRE METHUEN
and
TQ PUBLICATIONS

First published in Great Britain
1980
Eyre Methuen Ltd, 11 New Fetter Lane, London EC4P 4EE
and TQ Publications, 31 Shelton Street, London WC2H 9HT

Copyright © Colin Chambers 1980

ISBN
Eyre Methuen 0 413 46880 1 (paperback)
TQ Publications 0 904844 32 2 (hardback)

PN
2596
.S8
C44
1980

/ 39,552

Phototypeset in 10 on 11 point English Times by Carlinpoint Limited,
31 Shelton Street, London WC2H 9HT, and printed in Great Britain
by Edward Fox and Son Limited, Stratford-upon-Avon

Contents

Foreword

Other Spaces grew out of a wish to write about Buzz Goodbody, a Communist and feminist who killed herself in 1975, aged 28, having worked her entire professional life for the Royal Shakespeare Company (RSC). She was not remarkable because of her suicide — sadly there have been other suicides among young people working in theatre, such as the playwright John Mackendrick, who was associated with the National Theatre. Nor was the interest solely in her work, undervalued though it has been. I wanted to see how she had acted as a bridge between the values of the fringe and the traditions of the RSC — a mix that led to the opening of The Other Place and later The Warehouse. The book became, then, the story of those two 'other spaces'.

There is surprisingly little written about the way a company such as the RSC works. I could not have pieced together my story without the help of more than seventy people whom I interviewed for the book, and to whom I say 'thank you'. They ranged from actors, directors, designers and production workers to writers, researchers, administrators, and friends and relatives of Buzz Goodbody. Although the conclusions in the book are mine, I am indebted to them all, but in particular to: a group comprising Marcelle Goodbody, Ben Kingsley, Patrick Stewart, and Sue Todd, who helped get the project going; Ed Buscombe, Alan Dale, Sue Dommett, Alison Fell, Jan Mallinder, Gordon Parsons, and Mike Prior; directors Bill Alexander, John Barton, Peter Brook, John Caird, Penny Cherns, Ron Daniels, Howard Davies, Terry Hands, David Jones, Barry Kyle, Trevor Nunn, Clifford Williams; actors Sheila Allen, Peggy Ashcroft, George Baker, Tony Church, Paola Dionisotti, Ian McKellen, Bob Peck, and the late Andre van Gyseghem; designers Chris Dyer, Tazeena Firth, Ralph Koltai, Di Seymour, and Kit Surrey; writers (too many to name); and from the RSC in other capacities, George Barnaby, Cicely Berry, David Brierley, Maurice Daniels, Walter Donohue, Leo Leibovici, Genista McKintosh, Jean Moore, Bronwyn Robertson, Maggie Whitlum, and Bill Wilkinson.

This book is dedicated to the memory of Buzz Goodbody, and to all who take up her struggles.

Introduction

There was no great fuss when a corrugated iron hut was opened to the public in April 1974, 200 yards down the road from the grand Royal Shakespeare Theatre in Stratford-upon-Avon. National critics were not invited to the first production at The Other Place, which the director had aimed at Midlands school students rather than the arts page readers of the daily papers. Three years later, the Royal Shakespeare Company did bang the drum a bit to announce the opening of a similar venue in London, The Warehouse in Covent Garden, only a few minutes' walk from the RSC's main house, the Aldwych Theatre. By this time, however, The Other Place had been put firmly on the theatrical map. Within six months, The Warehouse was on that map too. Why did the RSC, with its immense reputation at home and abroad, open these two theatres in buildings not designed originally for public performance, and which between them seat at most 380 people? Why did those two small spaces not only sustain that reputation but also help it grow? The answers go deep and lie both inside and outside the RSC.

The fringe and the changing social fabric

While many people in the Company contributed to these developments, the crucial link in the chain was one particular director, Buzz Goodbody, who killed herself in 1975, aged 28. Inspired as she was by the radical cultural and political atmosphere of the 1960s, Buzz Goodbody became the catalyst for change within the RSC, the major subsidized company in Britain and arguably in the world. She provided the all-important bridge between the RSC and the fringe, combining its excitement and social challenge with the Company's classical strength and tradition of experiment.

The influence of the fringe is not easy to assess. It cannot be dismissed because it failed as an opposition: this was not surprising given the political situation. Artistic upheavals were more far-reaching in the wake of the First World War in, say, Germany, with its then unparalleled working-class organizations, and in the tumultuous Soviet Union. The fringe in Britain, with few exceptions, never had as strong a working-class base as did the agitprop groups or the mass pageants of the 1930s. But its effect as an alternative was widespread and it went deep.

Significant early manifestations of this influence included the 1967 visit of Café La Mama and the Open Theatre; the opening the

7

following year of the Arts Lab, which spawned the People Show, Pip Simmons, and the Freehold; Portable Theatre, and Marowitz's Open Space; Ed Berman's Inter-Action and its Other Company (directed by Naftali Yavin), exploring new relationships between actor, director, and audience; the Traverse in Edinburgh, with its workshop offering a new involvement for writers; the different combinations of left-wing theatre — Unity, Centre 42, CAST, Red Ladder; women's theatre, black theatre, gay theatre, theatre-in-education, physical theatre, community theatre, lunchtime theatre, and so on.

The spaces that were found by this contradictory, counter-cultural 'movement' expressed its ideology, economic situation, and social base. The Greeks had amphitheatres on the sides of mountains, reflecting the role of drama at the time, and the Austro-Hungarian emperors built vast opera houses, with rank and status defined in the architecture and placing of seats. The same sorts of relationship can be seen in Britain's theatres, from the eighteenth-century, ornate proscenium auditoria to the concrete, civic 1960s when theatres became complexes, or part of them, and were meant to reflect a democratic, supposedly classless, industrial welfare state.

The National and the RSC provided their own examples, with the RSC even choosing the symbolic heart of finance capital, the City, as its new home. The class reality, however, was shown in both cases by the fact that neither building was ready on time. But could such theatres be sustained anyway in a climate so different from that in which they were planned? The intention that the National's Olivier stage should present epic work springing from the community soon came to nothing. The social cohesion required for mass spectacle had gone, with no sign of any return in the near future. Loyalty to a club or the huge distribution network of a transnational record company could produce vast numbers for sport or rock music, but apart from summer shows and pantomime, which had become inseparable from the electronic entertainments, the audience for live theatre, especially in the capital or in Stratford, was so diverse as to make it difficult to achieve artistic coherence in a large auditorium: hence the turn to nostalgia, revivals of known 'favourites' — and, for Shakespeare, a generalized, rhetorical style.

It is no joke to play *Macbeth* to an audience of 1,600 seated in serried rows of plush seats whose view of the action is only as large as their purse, and which includes tourists who buy five tickets for twenty people — swopping at appropriate intervals so that they can all say they have seen English Shakespeare — some of whom cannot speak English, some who can but have never been to a theatre before. You are lucky if the audience gets the gist, let alone the meaning of the play.

8

The social base for the 'fringe' was, generally speaking, higher-educated, middle-class youth. Fed up with a hollow consumer society that paraded its false values everywhere, but unable to find any other society that inspired them, the 'existential, LSD, LP generation' wanted to overcome its alienation by making contact and by testing the truth for itself, as close as the television screen, as immediate, as disposable — but it had to be real. Truth was important, size was not. The universal, transcendental art of the affluent proscenium theatres had to be rejected like the class interests they serviced.

A radical spirit of equality was abroad which wanted to take theatre out of theatre buildings and onto the streets, into basements, halls, old churches, anywhere where there was space — even an ice rink. Anything that stood in the way of the basic purpose of theatre — to communicate — had to be stripped away. Theatres, including the two warlords, the RSC and the National Theatre, belonged to 'them', so the new spaces had to belong to 'us' and be part of the 'ordinary' world, because that was what theatre was all about — valuable in its own right and not because of the occasion. This impulse tied in physically and emotionally with the puritan tradition of non-conformist dissent: just as there was no authority between God and the believer, there had to be nothing between the performance and the audience, all of whom had to be equal. Each action was a moral problem, and this gave back to theatre its social role.

All the relationships of the theatre had to be changed and divisions of labour broken down. Theories of the 'poor theatre' and the 'empty space' came into vogue. The difference was not one of scale, but of philosophy. Later, when studios were incorporated into the 'mainstream', which had been changed by that process, the small was worshipped for itself as was the 'new', and was defined simply in relation to a 'main house'. This obscured the point, especially as some small spaces had acting areas as large as those of 'main' theatres (the same happened in the film world, where a changing social base meant that cinemas were broken up into smaller units, like an Odeon or an ABC 1, 2, 3, 4). New work by definition is less likely to command large audiences at first than a classic, though this does not mean it cannot, nor that any individual new work has to be shunted off to a siding. However, the cash responsibility of the larger theatre in a two-theatre operation is always a great weight, suggesting that it is difficult to be adventurous while the company knows it is death not to be.

But the important thing about the 'new spaces' was the different relationship they made possible between the audience and the performance — that is, the nature of the experience both for those putting the show on and for those coming along to see it. The RSC did not suddenly wake up to this when the 'fringe' arose. It had known that perhaps only the front eight rows or so in the Royal Shakespeare Theatre at Stratford could get that sort of contact, and then it was only a one way process, as the actors have to play to all the house. The Company tried many ways to get over the problem, from reconstructing the proscenium to actors crossing the 'footlights', as in Brook's *Dream* or in Bogdanov's *Shrew*, in which a traditional proscenium set was destroyed on stage. The RSC stopped short of taking the buildings down and starting again, but this search was one reason for wanting to move to a new theatre in the City.

However, the proscenium is not evil, just as the small spaces are not inherently good. Work of value or of none can be produced in either. It may be harder to get the truth in a proscenium, but then it is also easier to cheat. But the proscenium does come from a previous society whose values are no longer a driving force for progress, and on its own the limitations would have hindered the all-round development of the RSC, which is why the Company has always used small and flexible spaces. Buzz Goodbody reflected these concerns, and, having been involved in many of the RSC's small-scale projects since she joined in 1967, as well as being deeply influenced by the 'fringe', she was in a unique position to open the second Stratford auditorium, The Other Place.

The character and commitment of Buzz Goodbody
Born Mary Ann Goodbody in north London in 1946, she only later came to be known by the affectionate yet appropriate nickname Buzz, which was coined by her brother John. She felt it was usefully 'unisex' in a man's world (the first letter she received from the RSC addressed her as Mr. Buzz Goodbody, and at least one reviewer referred to her as a 'him'). Highly educated — at Francis Holland School, north London; at Roedean, the exclusive girls' school; and as the youngest undergraduate of her year at the new Sussex University (from 1964 to 1967) — she came from a cultured upper middle-class background, and as a student she had her first taste of working on classics and contemporary plays with a low budget, performing anywhere but in a theatre (the university did not then have a purpose-built auditorium), from the Physics Department courtyard to the college snack bar. Her adaptation of Dostoevsky's *Notes from Underground* was first staged in the Biology Lecture Hall, using chicken wire for the set instead of wood, which was too dear, and with a bigger cast than at the National Student Drama Festival in Cardiff, where it won a special £50 award for enterprise. These experiences stayed with her during her RSC days, helping to shape her method and approach to work, and were crucial in the thinking behind The Other Place.

10

When it came to setting up the new theatre, though, she felt many other pressures that had been generated from within the RSC, like her fear that the second auditorium would never get off the ground, and that after almost seven years she would not 'make it' with the Company. This would only prove, to those who wanted to see it, that a woman could not be as good a director as a man. She felt the RSC encouraged the feeling that it was the centre of the world. The stakes were high, there was a strong sense of internal competition, and failure could make you feel like a nobody. No-one else below leadership level had stayed as long as her, but despite advice from many inside and outside the RSC to leave and work in a regional theatre or in the 'fringe', she wanted to stay and scale the heights — to show that 'it could be done'.

She had often been on the verge of leaving. Her contracts never gave her security, and there were periods of unemployment or 'waiting for something to turn up' at the RSC when she would read scripts or take some understudy work for the Company — part of its 'cheap labour' system that is the lot of young or new directors. She had thoughts, like many others at the time, of running a theatre group from the back of a lorry, and even approached a theatre consultantcy about it. In 1968, she explored the idea of starting a small community theatre with a permanent company of actors. It was to be run with five friends, including her husband (with whom she split up the following year), writer Mike Stott, who was then helping the literary manager of the RSC, and Mike Leigh, whom she had met when she first joined the Company, and who was a great influence on her.

The scheme, which, Leigh says, 'serviced our fantasies', was dropped in 1970, the year Buzz Goodbody helped start The Women's Street Theatre Group, Britain's first feminist theatre company. She took part in its opening show, *Sugar and Spice,* in March 1971, despite a ban by the Department of the Environment because it was part of the first Women's Liberation march that was to end up in Trafalgar Square. She could be seen brandishing a huge deodorant, which she used to teach her 'daughter' the 'delights' of being 'feminine', dancing down Oxford Street with the group to the sound of Eddie Cantor singing 'Keep Young and Beautiful if You Want to be Loved' played on a tape in an old pram. The group returned to the theme of conditioning and stereotyping in later shows, like the one for a north London local festival in which Buzz Goodbody wore a black satin slip, put rollers in her hair, and shaved her legs in an imaginary boudoir on a float.

Goodbody was arrested and fined with the group at the Festival of Light when they presented a horrific tableau of family life with a placard saying 'Fuck the F*mily'. She also appeared in *Parade of Cats* by Jane Wibberley, the last play in a lunchtime season of women's theatre at the Almost Free, in which she parodied her appearance with Joan Bakewell on BBC's *Late Night Line Up* in a sketch about a career cat. She enjoyed the company's democratic, collective methods of work, which she could never fully implement at the RSC. She shared all the tasks, whether acting, painting, making props, producing publicity, or going through the painful but useful experience of jointly writing a script. A lot of the time, the company acted as her consciousness-raising group.

As a director with the RSC, Buzz Goodbody felt the disadvantage of being a woman in an overwhelmingly male Company, run, however sympathetically, by men. The RSC 'culture' had a sexual side to it, which is difficult to define, but — taking a cue from the images presented in productions by leading actresses — it stressed an erotic, Cleopatra type, with wit, strength of character, and an educated intelligence — a smart but casual grammar-school heterosexuality. The RSC was used to women in front of audiences or typewriters, taking voice or dancing classes, casting or planning, making wigs, hats, and costumes, but on the rehearsal floor it was a different matter. Buzz Goodbody blamed herself when things went wrong, and felt that if she were successful they would say, 'what a good director', but if a failure, 'the woman can't do it'.

She was the first and only woman director at the RSC, although Penny Cherns and Jane Howell have both directed one show each since. The 'fringe' has helped increase the number of woman directors, provided better opportunities for women at all levels, and focused attention on the problems facing women in a profession with high unemployment and no nursery provisions or protection for women. But it still takes five times as long for a woman to get the same experience as a man, and the power structure of the theatre has stayed the same as far as women are concerned.

The cheerful, bouncy Buzz would keep parts of herself private and well guarded, showing different sides of her personality to different people, but never the whole. She did not advertise her political affiliation, though she never denied it. Few in the RSC knew she was a member of the Communist Party, which she felt did not always take her work seriously, while many in the RSC who did see her running off to meetings thought she was mad. She found no satisfactory answer as to how she could be an active and useful party member as well as a round-the-clock theatre director. However, there were those in both organizations who did support her — as did the people she helped to write, lay out, and sell a local community 'free press' newspaper in north London.

By the time she came to open The Other Place, she had become part of the RSC, knowing and reproducing its ways and language, but at the same time resisting its capacity to absorb. She brought to bear her own values — drawn from the women's movement, the left, and the communal household in which she lived in London. This was invaluable for her, but she could not cope with the contradictions she faced about her work, her personal life, and her sexuality — her need for independence and security, her rejection of monogamy and the nuclear family while wanting a close, loving environment.

The legacy of Buzz Goodbody

Apart from the RSC, Buzz Goodbody never worked for any other company except the street theatre group, and directing a Sunday-night show at the Royal Court. She served a necessary and long apprenticeship under the different styles of John Barton, Terry Hands, and Trevor Nunn. She took risks, swinging between showbiz 'pop' pastiche and the hard-headed radical realism that left its mark on The Other Place. Her open-minded, magpie approach, using anything that was useful, helped her create volatile rehearsals in which actors felt pushed, but able to look at themselves and to work closely on a text in a practical and precise way from their own experience rather than through analogy, whether they were playing sympathetic characters or not. Her way of freeing actors to find out for themselves, though along lines she had laid down, made a unique impact (which they readily acknowledge) on many actors, including Sheila Allen, George Baker, Tony Church, Ben Kingsley, and Patrick Stewart.

But the cost to her was always high. She lived out on the rehearsal floor her own ambiguities, her desperation and her joy, her insecurities and her ambitions, her commitment and her search for purpose. Though not a substitute for a political party, working on a production for her was a political act, from the scrupulous research into the text, its imagery, structure, and social background, to the exploration of the relationships between the characters. Tense and intense, she was constantly focusing on the connections between the political, the family and the state. Rather like the Italian film-makers of the 1960s, her productions told exciting stories which were about ideas only in so far as they were lived by and between people who were recognizable and faced similar problems to the audience. She bridged the classical and the modern, the alternative and the mainstream, by heightening a tradition instead of breaking it. 'Unless classical theatre becomes the property of the whole of society', she said, 'it will atrophy'. She did not rebel against the idea of theatre, but faced the long-term challenge of closing the culture gap through the mixed repertoire of The Other Place.

Like many directors who have to act all kinds of roles to keep the members of a cast happy, she was emotionally raw, and bottled up more of herself than a man might have done, so as to 'prove' that a woman could be just as 'rational'. She judged herself harshly against her contemporaries and always feared that The Other Place would be closed. She even inquired about doing a Ph.D. at Cambridge after finishing *Hamlet*. She was haunted by the memory of finding the body of an actor on the RSC tour of Australia who had committed suicide, and by a dream of smashing into a tree after a high-speed car ride. The suicide of the RSC's youngest and only woman director was a willed act, planned some time beforehand.

Tributes came from unexpected quarters, like American students and the Institute of Workers Control. A tree was planted in her honour by the Rotunda in Stratford, across the road from The Other Place, and a Sunday-evening concert was given by many colleagues at the Aldwych in December 1975 to remember her and to set up a fund for an annual Buzz Goodbody Award to be presented to a director at the National Union of Students/*Sunday Times* Drama Festival. Pam Gems also remembered her in the part of Fish in *Dusa, Fish, Stas and Vi,* written before her death but amended afterwards. Buzz Goodbody had represented the hopes and disillusions of the 1960s coming to terms with the 1970s, feeling politically and artistically isolated and betrayed as a woman.

But it was her kind of approach that proved the most resilient and productive in the new decade, not that of groups like Mnouchkine's Le Théâtre du Soleil, which performed *1789* in the Roundhouse in 1971 to prophecies of a new dramatic era. (Ironically, the other main advocate of 'chamber classics', Jonathan Miller, took an opposite view of their purpose. To him, small meant élite whereas, for Goodbody, it was only the start of a long haul to bring theatre in line with new developments in society.) She did not dismiss the theatre as middle class, because she recognized the importance of that class and its culture — in which theatre, and particularly the RSC, plays a crucial role. She did not see theatre or culture as above politics or socially neutral, but full of contradictions which she hoped to resolve artistically from what might be described as a progressive, democratic perspective, opening up her work to more rather than less people, while remaining honest to her own views. She was learning at every step, achieving more deeply and consistently her changing artistic vision, which The Other Place only partly expressed, but which lives on in the work of actors, designers, directors, and production staff whom she influenced and who influenced her.

1. The structural background: the nature of the RSC

Events in the years leading up to the opening of The Other Place had been among the most volatile since the Second World War. Vietnam, Czechoslovakia, China, Ireland, Berkeley, Paris, Chicago — the flashpoints have become the commonplace of political analysis. New battlegrounds and new battlecries emerged that touched every aspect of life. All were deeply democratic, whether in the organized working-class militancy against a state attack unparalleled since the 1920s, or the far-reaching challenges of the women's movement. For the RSC, this period, which saw the 'fringe' or 'alternative' explosion, coincided with the difficult, first years under Trevor Nunn, who had taken over in 1968 as artistic director from Peter Hall at the age of 28.

Struggles for subsidy, pressures of status

Apart from the obvious problem of following a man of Hall's stature, and in the Company he had created, Nunn inherited a financial crisis and commitments to artists which he had to reconcile with his own plans for where the RSC should be going and how it should be getting there. Yet Nunn soon learnt the ropes. He and the administrative and artistic group that helped him survived with tremendous hard work. They scored critical successes, broke their own world-beating box-office records, won several new shelf-fulls of international awards, and increased output and productivity. They made a sensible adjustment to the RSC's two-theatre, two-year operation through the introduction of a two-year contract, with a smaller company playing a longer season and providing fuller understudy cover of a higher quality, and through improved use of the Aldwych.

But it all took its toll, not least on the health of those at the top, and the RSC reached danger point. Even in 1968 it had been dubbed 'the ICI of the theatre', and since then had fallen even more into line with the industrial logic of capitalism. The Company was starting to do too much, and not as well as it might. Hall, championing an ensemble philosophy, had broken the competitive star system of the 1950s, and had established a national company on a permanent basis with a strong identity both for its public and for itself. But, just as the hopes pinned to Labour in the same period were to be dashed, the artistic and democratic thrust of the ensemble's egalitarian 'collective exploration', in achieving new successes, gave rise to new stars and

15

new distinctions of status within the Company.

It could hardly have been otherwise, as the fight for subsidy, though temporarily won, did not, and could not, mean the end of a mixed theatrical economy and the hand-to-mouth survival that it demands. The RSC could have chosen other ways of meeting that situation but, once having taken its decisions, the management worked to its brief with outstanding efficiency. The trouble was that growth had become the yardstick for success, the books had to balance, and the RSC had become (though in less acute a form), like the nationalized industries, a slave to the profit motive. If the Company were to avoid turning into a Shakespeare museum, then it had to find a way of holding and attracting artists and technicians who could present a repertoire that expressed the views held by Nunn and others in the leadership — that is, of a theatre that was socially perceptive and relevant to new audiences drawn from a wider social background.

But in a worsening economic situation, the RSC also had to keep its theatres open. In 1974, a record number of productions and new activities still left a deficit that put survival in doubt. The crisis threatened to close the Aldwych and saw the suspension there in 1975 of the repertoire system. Believing the best form of defence to be attack, the artistic response was the opening of The Other Place in Stratford and, the logical next step, the opening of The Warehouse in London. Expansion and diversity continued, to match the Company's philosophy — in particular the search for new audiences. RSC press releases boasted of ever mightier achievements. The seasons in Newcastle, which the Company had hoped would become a third centre of operation — and which arguably has since become so — started in March 1977 and became part of the regular RSC calendar, involving work from both the large and the small theatres. Out of the latter came the small-scale tours to towns and villages that either had no live theatre or were rarely visited by a company like the RSC.

These successes, which tackled the crisis caused by growth and yet were only possible because of that growth, strengthened that same process of expansion, which hit its next crisis in 1979-80. Whereas the RSC could renew itself in the early 1970s, when social and political movement, ideas, energy, and excitement were in the air, and the 'fringe' and the colleges were active, by the close of the decade these sources had run dry as the country's problems were being tackled with increasingly right-wing solutions. However, the renewal of the 1970s was remarkable, both artistically and organizationally. Equivalent to a medium-size business enterprise, with over 500 people on its books at any one time, the Company was a model Arts Council client. It earned a higher proportion of what it spent than any comparable institution, and brought in a lot of foreign currency. There was no

16

increase in administrative, box office, or publicity staff to match the expansion in output. Existing resources were ably exploited, while the RSC adapted nimbly in a business full of risks caused by the conditions of the marketplace. Here, the audiences became the consumers, subject to whim and rising prices of tickets, travel, and eating out; the 'producers' of the goods were mainly artists in a highly insecure profession, and its funding was a mixture — of insufficient public money granted year by year, which makes planning difficult, and of private sponsorship, which necessarily can only satisfy a need in the theatre when that coincides with the operations of the market.

The theatre is also particularly vulnerable to inflation as the gap between income and expenditure widens. It is a labour-intensive industry, using luxury materials in its costumes and sets and having less power to get back the money (especially when the government cuts its grant), because there is an obvious limit on the raising of prices already augmented by Value Added Tax. The RSC was deft at encouraging commercial sponsors — its first small-scale tour in 1978 could not be funded by the Company, but was mounted through backing from a greetings-cards firm that won the first award for business sponsorship of the arts. But the RSC never believed that this could, or should, replace a substantial and regular grant from the public purse. In 1980 it was considering the appointment of a sponsorship officer.

Authority, devolution, and the need for renewal

One of the main reasons for the RSC's success as an organization has been the strength and continuity of its 'culture' — that is, its own standards, values, and ways of doing things. Hall's 'ensemble', loose enough to embrace almost everyone he needed and led by crusading individuals, gave way to a more corporate Company. More power was concentrated at the top and responsibility was 'devolved' further. The metaphor that still occurs is that of the family, and the traditional implications hold true. The Company remains a male-dominated hierarchy, with those who are definitely parents and those who are definitely children (and if they happen to be secretaries and women, which is most often the case, they will be servicing their wise, humanist 'fathers' with cups of tea or coffee). The family asks for and expects loyalty, but looks after those it considers its own, especially in dealing with 'outsiders' like the Arts Council. It is riven by rows, and a lot depends on personality, though in public the family keeps face.

Thus, when one of the governors broke the code in 1964, complaining in public that the RSC was putting on 'dirty plays', he and those who supported him were severely rebuffed. The board has

17

kept mum since, mainly because the books have been balanced (though a Conservative MP did resign in 1972 because he thought the RSC too left-wing).

No family would see the need for an industrial relations department, and neither does the RSC. Instead, day-to-day affairs are regulated by 'house' agreements with the unions covering actors, musicians, and production staff (from cleaners to stage hands) but not administrative staff (unlike the National). The relationships the different sections have with the family is expressed in their contracts — the most distinctive being the arrangements with actors, and notably with the 'associate artists' who can establish a long-term relationship with the RSC while remaining 'free' to take on other work. Individual actors can carry weight, depending on who they are, as can a cast if there is widespread feeling on an issue, but Company meetings have become more a means of passing on information than a channel for active democracy. Two leading actors were taken onto the planning committee in 1979, while the elected company committees (which meet whenever they want and usually with whichever member of the permanent staff is responsible for whatever is being discussed) have little or no power. They are useful for 'letting off steam', which can help head off a challenge to management, or for bringing issues to management before they 'get out of hand', but as with most decision-making beneath the top level it is a matter of 'how', not 'whether'.

At the top, which is divided between managers and directors, it has been important to keep the 'culture' healthy in order to hold the Company together as it expanded. Devolution became crucial to the renewal as authority became more centralized. The family has two main offspring, Stratford and London, each with its own identity within the RSC 'culture', and both have a large and a small theatre, each with its own identity. This has meant that the RSC can let certain of its 'offspring' have their head as long as they bring home the bacon. Manageable units have also made budget control easier, and multiplied the dividends. (The same pattern began to emerge at the National, which had to cope all at once with one big unit, and then tried to set up a different company for each of its three auditoria.) Disagreements between members of the family about their identity or even about the overall 'culture' itself are kept from pulling the RSC apart by the 'culture' itself, by the ultimate power of the chief executive, under the governors, and by the practical need each has for the other — all the operations being dependent on each other and fitting together in terms of available resources. The strain on the artistic 'parents' of keeping the family together can be enormous, besides distracting them away from the business of directing plays.

In this respect, the nature of the Company is difficult to assess by conventional 'bums-on-seats' thinking — as are all those factors that go toward putting the bums there, bringing them back, or keeping them away. How do you estimate the role of The Other Place or The Warehouse in building the image of the RSC in the 1970s — separately, that is, from their earning power, which will always be minute by comparison with the larger theatres? Certainly the smaller theatres have contributed dynamically to the RSC 'culture', playing an important role artistically in keeping the Company to its own standards with resilience and determination in the face of a weak, mixed economy.

2. The historical background: early experiments in 'other spaces'

As the RSC is based on Shakespeare, its ability to adapt and renew itself depends on how it presents his works. This had been linked to the idea of cross-fertilization between the classic and the contemporary from the beginnings of Peter Hall's artistic direction, when — at the age of 29, and under the influence of the continental two-theatre complex — he opened a London venue for the RSC at the Aldwych Theatre. Here, it was intended to present a mixed repertoire, including foreign companies (which in 1964 led to Peter Daubeny's first World Theatre Season). The cross-fertilization theory was rooted in the belief that an artist needs the edge of modern ideas to cut through all that lies between Shakespeare and a modern audience, while also needing to bring the experience of handling Shakespeare — especially his language and structure — to new work which has no comparable tradition. Despite not working as neatly as this, the impetus behind it, linked to the complementary drive to get new audiences in front of new Shakespeare, did shape a tradition within the RSC that led to the setting up of The Other Place.

'Other spaces' in the sixties

In 1962, Hall had invited two innovators, Peter Brook and Michel Saint-Denis, to join him. It was the year of the RSC's experimental season at the 350-seat Arts Theatre, where Hall had directed the British premiere of *Waiting for Godot* in 1955. This season fed into the sequence of adapted history plays, *The Wars of the Roses,* in 1963, and was remarkable for those it brought together and for the work they presented. There were two neglected 'classics' — Middleton's *Women Beware Women* (1621), directed by Anthony Page, who was later to run the Royal Court, and Gorky's *The Lower Depths* (1902), directed by Toby Robertson, who was to run the touring Prospect, which later inherited the mantle of the Old Vic Company; two plays by 'known' but risky writers — the stylized and metaphorical *Everything in the Garden,* by Giles Cooper, which was directed by Donald McWhinnie, the influential BBC producer and promoter of the absurd dramatists who was then an RSC associate director, and the rough, choppy, farcical *Nil Carborundum* by Henry Livings, directed by Anthony Page; *The Empire Builders,* by an almost unheard-of French iconoclast Boris Vian, who had died in 1959, directed by David Jones, who was to become an associate director of the RSC; and finally, two new plays that could only be played in a club theatre because of the censor — David Rudkin's *Afore Night Come,* directed by Clifford Williams, who had joined the RSC the year before and was to become an associate the following year, and *Infanticide in the House of Fred Ginger* by Fred Watson, directed by William Gaskill, who was to run the Royal Court later with Page. But although the actors, writers, and designers as well as the directors, represented the major influences of the late 1950s, financial problems prevented the continuation of the Arts experiment, and the cosmopolitan mix at the Aldwych continued, with two programmes — *Expeditions One* (1964) and *Expeditions Two* (1965) — providing outlets for innovative small-scale work.

Only the charismatic Brook sustained the experimental strand, working 'in public' — while Saint-Denis, who was not in good health at this time, mainly did studio work 'in private', though his influence on policy was important. Brook's development took him from *The Theatre of Cruelty* season of 1964 with Charles Marowitz at LAMDA and the Donmar Theatre (later to become The Warehouse) to the *Marat/Sade* in the Aldwych's most successful season of new work, and on to *The Investigation* (1965) and *US* (1966), both at the Aldwych, and *A Midsummer Night's Dream* (1970) at Stratford — and so to Paris and his 'universal' theatre research, and away from that 1962 *King Lear,* which hung over the 'swinging sixties' like a warning cloud.

If Brook was a link with the Stratford forerunners of the RSC, Saint-Denis was a bridge to a rich European tradition going back to the 1920s, which included his own Compagnie des Quinze of acrobatic pioneers, the London Theatre Studio, the Old Vic and its post-war theatre school, and leading personalities like Tyrone Guthrie, George Devine, John Gielgud, and Laurence Olivier. Saint-Denis founded the RSC's Actors Studio when he joined the Company (which is empowered by its Charter to run a drama school), working in a tent on the lawn at Stratford before a corrugated iron hut was built for him, 200 yards down the road from the main theatre — later to become The Other Place. His approach laid great stress on the visual, and he brought into the Company Farrah, the head of design at the Strasbourg School of which Saint-Denis had been director. His work was seen by the leadership as integral to the Company's life — a workshop for actors, directors, writers, designers, and technical staff, to develop singly and together their own craft and imagination, and that of the Company, as a company.

This was necessary to build the artistic framework required by an ensemble without making everyone a prisoner of that security. Classes were held in many skills — dancing, speech, singing, fencing, wrestling, improvisation, acrobatics, and mask work. The voluntary sessions were fitted into the working day as best they could be, and took place anywhere from a dressing room to the circle bar — and led to 'internal' one-act productions, like Genet's *Deathwatch*. Separate from Saint-Denis, who understandably refused to touch Shakespeare because of the language problem, the studio work was used to look at Shakespeare's verse and to find ways of revealing it to a modern audience. This was the basis for the RSC's distinctive achievement in the 1960s, which owed a great deal to the expertise in Elizabethan verse and drama of John Barton, whom Hall brought in from Cambridge University at the very start of his work with the Company.

The Theatregoround years

The other side of this coin was the search for the modern audience. In March 1965, a group of actors sponsored by the RSC's Members' Club, which organized special events and ran a newspaper called *Flourish*, put together a programme of brief shows taken from Shakespeare, modern plays, and other writings, to tour halls and canteens — and included was a talk with the audiences after the performance. By September, the shows had lengthened to 90 minutes and the group had grown to include six actors. It had a name, Theatregoround (TGR), and under Michael Kustow it visited working-class London boroughs and took its first play, Shaw's *On the Rocks,* to the Isle of Dogs in the East End. TGR moved to Stratford in June 1966, touring Midlands schools with Barton's teaching/learning programme about *Henry V — The Battle of Agincourt,* the first small-scale work on Shakespeare the Company had done.

TGR brought live theatre to schools, youth clubs, colleges, community centres, housing estates, and factories, accompanied often by a mobile exhibition, the Show Bus, which was linked to the varied programme. This included many demonstration performances like *The Actor at Work* or *The Actor and the Director,* scenes from plays to show different styles of acting and approaches to theatre, teachers' courses, and educational pieces like *The Trial and Execution of Charles I,* which was linked to a commercial 'kit' of documents and material about the period that schools could use in class.

Such anthologies were the staple, but by no means exclusive diet. They included *Pleasure and Repentance, Eve and After, Room for Company, Men at Arms, When Thou Art King, The Merry Month of May,* and the grandparent of them all, *The Hollow Crown,* which had started life as a one-night filler at the Aldwych in 1961 and remained in the RSC repertoire ever since. Plays ranged from *The Proposal* to

Waiting for Godot, from *The Dumb Waiter* to *Volpone, Two Gentlemen of Verona, Under Milk Wood, US,* and two pieces by the off-off-Broadway writer Lanford Wilson. In 1970 Nunn brought TGR under central control because he felt it was becoming too autonomous, and though this had produced more work (fourteen performances a week on average in 100 different venues one year), it had also meant that the TGR group was spending too much time away from the parent Company. Nunn felt that this disrupted the philosophy and put standards in danger. He thought the answer was more small-scale classics and tried to co-ordinate the casting and design of TGR with the main theatre. He extended the Stratford season to include TGR productions (*King John* and *Dr. Faustus* in 1970, and in TGR's last year, 1971, *Henry V* and *Richard II* — the forerunner of the production under Barton two years later, when Richard Pasco and Ian Richardson alternated the roles of Richard and Bolingbroke).

At the end of 1970, TGR staged a festival in the Roundhouse in London, which had been used the year before to run children's workshops under Marjorie Sigley. A new production, *Arden of Faversham,* was joined by *John* and *Faustus,* and there were open rehearsals and discussions. Three other Stratford shows (*Hamlet, Richard III,* and *The Dream*) were played without décor and costume, to 'encourage a creative and close actor/audience relationship', according to one of the programme notes. There was no consensus within the RSC on the role of TGR, which changed over the years. Its missionary side appealed to many in theory but few in practice, and there was a resistance to being parachuted into a community with a morsel of 'art' as bait — or a substitute — for the 'real thing' in Stratford or London.

TGR productions were mostly performed by 'juniors' (apart from *The Hollow Crown*), until the last two years when the shows went into the Royal Shakespeare Theatre. This 'second eleven' feel made some think of it as a penance, though for others it was a way of staying sane when you were stuck in Stratford with little to do once the main productions had opened. Many enjoyed the independence from what was a hierarchical acting company, going out 'on the road' and often without a director. In 1968, *The Hollow Crown* and *Under Milk Wood* went to Belfast 'on their own', though usually the geographical limit was set by the need to get back to 'base' for a performance. A group emerged committed to the useful work of TGR, especially in overcoming the notion — held strongly within the Company then — that their craft was a mystery that had to be guarded from outsiders.

Some of this group went on to form Actors in Residence, which toured colleges, often in the US, performing Shakespeare and talking

23

about those performances and about the profession in general. Money for TGR at first came from an anonymous £10,000 donation, and was followed by funds from sources such as the Calouste Gulbenkian Foundation and the Midland Red Bus Company, but it was not long before the operation, including an artistic director and small staff, came completely under the RSC budget. The Arts Council would never fund TGR or increase the RSC grant to cover it; on the contrary, there was pressure to drop it altogether — a situation which repeated itself later in the setting up of The Other Place and The Warehouse.

From The Place to The Other Place

When it was obvious that TGR was taking too big a slice of the RSC cake, the Company was determined not to lose all that had been learnt from it: the disciplines of flexible, low-budget, small-cast, small-space productions and, in particular, the experiences of the Festival in the Roundhouse. In the autumn of 1971 the RSC hired The Place, the headquarters of the Contemporary Dance Theatre off the Euston Road, for a nine-week season of new work, which opened with Buzz Goodbody's production of *Occupations,* the first full-length play by the then little-known Trevor Griffiths. This was followed by Robert Montgomery's play with music, *Subject to Fits,* loosely based on Dostoevsky's *The Idiot,* Strindberg's *Miss Julie,* and, as an afterthought, late-night performances of *The Oz Trial.*

The auditorium had been specially designed to seat 330 people on ₹ raked bank in-the-round (or three-quarters round). Tickets were cheap (90p), and the audience could sit anywhere. The RSC used The Place again in 1973 for a new-play season — *Cries from Casement as His Bones are Brought to Dublin* by David Rudkin, *Section Nine* by Philip Magdalany, *Hello and Goodbye* by Athol Fugard, *Sylvia Plath* devised by Barry Kyle, and *A Lesson in Blood and Roses* by John Wiles — and in the following year, when *Lear* transferred from The Other Place to play alongside Strindberg's *Comrades,* an English version by Charles Wood of Victor Lanoux's *The Can Opener,* and Snoo Wilson's *The Beast.*

In Stratford, aspects of the internal studio work had continued after Saint-Denis had withdrawn from active life in the Company in 1966 (though he remained a consultant director until his death in 1971). The so-called Conference Hall, a rehearsal space behind the stage in the Royal Shakespeare Theatre (RST), had been used for studio work and 'extra-mural' activities since 1964, when Tony Church directed *The Second Shepherd's Play* there after all the main productions had opened. During this end-of-season 'flare-up', as it was called, you

24

could keep on your toes, earn your spurs, or let your hair down, either without set or costumes, or with whatever you could beg, steal, or borrow.

New methods of staging Greek drama were tried (anticipating John Barton's classical sequence, *The Greeks,* in 1980), as were new plays (or often just scenes), one-acters, or short versions of plays, to let as many as possible have a chance to do something — particularly the walk-ons, stand-ins, or understudies. In 1970 a group formed around actors Martin Bax and Hugh Keays Byrne, and took the name Chaff and Bran (from a line by Pandarus referring to foot soldiers). They converted a rotunda in the gardens behind the main theatre into an auditorium and called it the Little Roundhouse (it became a brass rubbing centre when the theatrical activities moved across the way to the corrugated iron hut). Here, in 1971 as well, they put on all sorts of shows, including revues, poetry readings, an hour-long *Macbeth,* a programme on the Spanish poet Lorca, and a satire on Peter Brook compering the Eurovision Song Contest played in front of the great man himself.

In 1972 there was no season in London at The Place, and the company playing *The Romans* in Stratford missed the TGR outlet. Nunn had been impressed by London 'fringe' theatres such as the Kings Head, the Royal Court Theatre Upstairs, and the Open Space (where some actors from the RSC presented Howard Brenton's *Gum and Goo* at lunchtime in 1970, having performed it 'internally' in the RSC's London rehearsal rooms). Under pressure from the actors, Nunn saw possibilities for the Saint-Denis hut which, like many temporary buildings, had remained *in situ* as TGR base and offices, a TGR course centre, and for rehearsals and storage. As the RSC announced another London season at The Place for 1973, the leaking hut in Stratford, with puddles on the floor and an out-of-tune piano, was to have a short run to test its usefulness as a theatre. A public performance licence was obtained and benches without backs were put in to seat 180, leaving a playing area of from eighteen to twenty square yards.

In June, two new assistant directors presented their own projects. Barry Kyle staged Sylvia Plath's only play, *The Three Women,* after a short tour; with added biographical material, this became *Sylvia Plath,* and transferred to London. Patrick Tucker directed *Christopher Columbus* and *Escurial* by Michel de Ghelderode. Both programmes were sold out, and the trial run convinced Nunn that there was a future for The Studio Theatre, as it was called — the red sign over its door complete with white swan — and that the RSC could cope with logistical problems like dovetailing the casts between this theatre and the RST. He suggested to the RSC planning committee that The Studio Theatre should be kept going for one more year at least, and that its artistic director should be Buzz Goodbody. The planning committee asked her to draw up a document with recommendations before any decisions were taken.

3. The personal background: the pioneering role of Buzz Goodbody

The renewal of the RSC in the 1970s came through its 'other spaces', and when Buzz Goodbody opened The Other Place her role was to give voice to a new set of concerns within the existing experimental tradition, and thereby to change it, opening the way for the generation of directors, designers, and actors from the fringe who became crucial to the Company.

Buzz Goodbody joins the RSC

Goodbody had herself joined the RSC in 1967, aged twenty, as John Barton's personal assistant. The RSC, with its first commitment to Shakespeare, has always had problems bringing on new and young directors. Hall had brought into the Company a new generation of actors and directors — like Trevor Nunn from Coventry and Terry Hands from Liverpool — but with the growth of regional theatre and the 'fringe', their contemporaries and the next generation either stayed with the 'alternative' theatre or, like Robin Phillips, Gareth Morgan, Nick Barter, Nick Young, Michael Rudman, and Mike Leigh, passed quickly through the RSC.

Brook had gone to Paris to get away from a situation he as much as anyone had helped create, where achievement had led to a treadmill and a heavy load for directors. The burden was carried by Nunn, Jones, and Hands — and by John Barton, who has never received the public acclaim of the other RSC directors, but whose influence has been as profound and vital to the RSC as any. It was Barton and not one of the younger three in the leadership who went in January 1967 to the Garrick Theatre in London's West End to see Dostoevsky's *Notes from Underground* in a triple bill from the twelfth National Union of Students/*Sunday Times* Drama Festival, and who went around to the stage door to offer the director a job. The director's name was Goodbody.

Barton was not looking for a 'nine-to-five typist', as he puts it. He was only interested in a 'Girl Friday' slave and companion, but university-trained, who was keen on the theatre, and Buzz was the first such 'dogsbody' whom Barton took on. She came to Stratford a rebel against her background, aware of prejudice against women though not then a feminist. She joined the Communist Party, and developed views that would later be described as 'Eurocommunist'.

Despite certain mutual sympathies, she and Barton had opposite characters and, against her better judgement, for eighteen months she put up with the shopping, the paper work, parking his car, getting his pills, and ironing his shirts. But she learnt a lot from him, and it offered her a way in to the prestigious company. However — and he made it clear — he was not going to promote her as a protégée. She assisted Barton on his two 1967 productions, *Coriolanus* and *All's Well That Ends Well;* with Theatregoround (TGR), for which she devised an anthology on the seven ages of women called *Eve and After;* on understudy work; and on 'internal' productions in the Conference Hall, including Genet's *The Maids* (in which she had acted at University), *King John,* Jonson's *Epicene,* and *Richard III.*

TGR's artistic director, Terry Hands, asked Barton if Buzz could help him on *The Merry Wives of Windsor,* seen at the Royal Shakespeare Theatre in 1968, and, in line with new, post-war attitudes to Shakespeare production, she did a great deal of research for him, especially on the class background of the play. While Hands worked on the text, she took improvisations based on her investigations of Hallowe'en and Celtic festivals, village life, and the rising bourgeoisie, soon to be victorious in the coming civil war, and this helped rescue the play from the roly-poly basket farce it had become. Instead, it was a lively piece of comic social realism.

Goodbody was made assistant director for the whole Stratford season in 1969 (*Henry VIII* and *The Winter's Tale* directed by Nunn, *Twelfth Night* by Barton, and, with Hands, *Women Beware Women, Pericles,* and a revival of *Merry Wives*). Each production was performed with a basic staging and lighting scheme designed by Christopher Morley, quickly characterized as a 'white box'. Again her painstaking academic preparation came in useful — the work on the social context of *Merry Wives* for *Women Beware Women,* and new research on the mask and the popular spectacle for the two late plays, which resulted in the sheep-shearers of Bohemia becoming Carnaby Street disco-dancers. Nunn, who had been impressed by the scenes she had directed from *John,* asked her to do a full Theatregoround production which would come into the RST.

The work for Theatregoround

Goodbody's TGR production of *King John* opened at the Nuffield Theatre, University of Southampton, in June 1970, and the press show for the national critics was held a week later at a cheap-price Saturday matinee. The savage response of some clouded the more encouraging reviews, particularly those of the local critics who are often more able to take less-than-perfect conditions in their stride.

John proved a success on tour, to the point in Corby where the manager said that if he could put on shows like that all the time, he would be a happy man for the rest of his life. *John* had not been seen in Stratford for thirteen years, and even the critics of the production agreed it was an 'uneven' play. But leaving aside the problems created by putting a small-scale show, conceived and designed for flexible, rough touring, into the 1,600-seater monster known locally as the Gaumont, and the fact that the director's imagination was at times running ahead of her technical means of expression, the production was still remarkable as an entertaining, refreshing, and original piece of Shakespeare that spoke directly to its modern audience. This, after all, is what the RSC conceived to be its purpose.

The set was simple, and had to be — a single sheet or screen as a backdrop. A lone percussion musician standing just in sight accompanied the action — banging a drum, for example, to mark an entrance or an exit, which, in the case of the King (Patrick Stewart) was like that of a puppet toy soldier, stiffly strutting, wearing a dunce's cap for a crown. Playing-card costumes completed the nursery atmosphere, signalled by a quotation from A. A. Milne in the programme — which also carried pictures of Edward Heath with a baby, Nixon, and Krushchev shaking hands with Mao. The production had broken with the patriotic, anti-French view of the play, which had been popular since the nineteenth century, and was instead a blistering attack on politicians, as if it had been written in 1970 by a Howard Brenton or a Howard Barker. Its preoccupation with the state of the nation torn apart through *Realpolitik,* cynical bargaining, and truces made and broken, struck a chord, especially as Britain was in the middle of the 1970 election campaign.

The key character in the play, which breaks with Shakespeare's chronicle cycle of histories, was seen as the Bastard (Norman Rodway). His speech beginning 'Mad world, mad kings, mad composition' — with its central reference to 'commodity, the bias of the world' — was the pivot of the interpretation. Here was an important voice of the 1970s, exploring the choice between the ineffectiveness of self-satisfied political isolation and the compromise of political engagement, a problem that figured in all of Goodbody's work, as well as in her life. Here at Stratford was the flavour of Littlewood, the living newspaper, a fast-moving, fluent, cartoon-strip production for all its faults, sardonic, grotesque — rolling Punch and Judy and a Plantagenet Ubu into one with the fun and excitement of sport. Here was the same mixture of Asiatic simplicity and western vulgarity that Brecht enjoyed (and which British audiences were again to applaud when the Georgian Rustaveli company performed *Richard III* in much the same style, at the Edinburgh Festival in 1979 and at the

Roundhouse in 1980). She had pushed the performances to the point of caricature, but, through respect for the text, had made the issues crystal clear.

The politics came through in a new way for an RSC production. Even with Peter Hall's *The Wars of the Roses* and its presentation of power struggles, RSC Shakespeare had still been far removed from the realities of contemporary conflict. But Goodbody had trodden on hallowed ground, had taken Shakespeare by the scruff of the neck, and had broken with the RSC's 'aesthetic' style. The result was neither the complete dismantling and reconstruction that Charles Marowitz was undertaking with his 'collage' versions of *Hamlet* and others, though the tone was similar; nor the radical transformation of Brook that would storm Stratford the same season with *The Dream*. Nevertheless, her *John* looked forward to the 1970s in a way that Brook did not. His was the effervescent celebration that marked the end of a dying decade which had seen a midsummer night's dream in the post-war period of capitalist decay. Hers was the social and political understanding of the post-1968 period, more clear-sighted and less spectacular. Brook, who was an inspiration for Buzz Goodbody, was 'taken by the vigour' of *John,* which he found 'full of life, energetic, disrespectful'. What would the critics have said if his name had been on the programme instead of an unknown woman's?

Goodbody's work for Theatregoround continued in London on preparations for the TGR festival to be held at the Roundhouse from October to December. She and Hands were working on a documentary about the General Strike of 1926, to be taken from the parliamentary reports of the time. This was more in line with what she wanted to do than literary anthologies — especially as she had undertaken the Japanese-Australian tour of *Merry Wives* and *Winter's Tale,* plus an anthology she had been asked to prepare called *To Be or Not to Be,* culled from nineteen Shakespeare plays, and with which she was not very happy. It was at this time that the national press first picked up the presence in the RSC of a woman director, when her name was listed in a release. An *Observer* reporter called her a 'leggy brunette in boots and a mini-skirt', while the *Sun*'s man, noting her penchant for peanut butter, 40 fags a day, Judy Collins, Bob Dylan, and the Beatles, also spotted the long legs and added that she was 'curvy, well-endowed in the right places'.

She spent twelve weeks researching *Strike*, which was to have songs by Guy Woolfenden and words by David Benedictus, who later staged a version of it in London called *What a Way to Run a Revolution.* Buzz Goodbody went to Scotland and the North-East to look for background material, talking to Labour Movement historians and veterans, including two militants who had been attached to the

Comintern. They lived in Chopwell, County Durham, known locally as 'Little Moscow', and Buzz Goodbody decided that this should be the focus of the play — what had happened there day-by-day, the setting fire to lorries, the problems of communications, the life at the union offices, the role of the parties. But the project did not gell. Nunn took over from Hands and wanted to turn the Roundhouse into a fairground with separate booths for different parts of the story. This idea fell apart because the production needed a ghost train which was too expensive to hire, though Farrah had done the designs, based on newsreels and photographs, and a programme looking like the TUC bulletin was ready.

Goodbody was rushed into filling the *Strike* slot by directing *Arden of Faversham,* a tragedy written in the early 1590s, often attributed, at least in part, to Shakespeare. Buzz Goodbody was keen on the play, which had been directed by Joan Littlewood in 1954, William Gaskill in 1961, and had been performed by Café La Mama in 1969 — a fine, progressive pedigree. But the conditions were bad and her terms of reference were different from those of the leading actress (which was to happen again in *As You Like It*), and she left two days before the show opened. Another director had to take the production through its final technical stages.

Occupations and The Oz Trial

In the first season at The Place, Goodbody was asked to direct Trevor Griffiths's *Occupations.* It had been performed already in Manchester, but Griffiths's agent had sent it to David Jones, who was in charge of the Aldwych, because of his RSC productions of O'Casey, Mercer, and Günter Grass's *The Plebeians Rehearse the Uprising* the year before — though the Company had found it too much of a risk in 1964. Times had changed, and the RSC was prepared to present a play about two views of revolution, which was set in the wake of the Bolshevik Revolution and Italy's post-war financial crisis, during the occupation of the Fiat factories by the workers of Turin in 1920. Times had not, however, changed quite enough for this Socialist play to be presented at the Aldwych, which that season had Joyce, Pinter, Genet, and Gorky in its repertoire.

Once more, Buzz Goodbody researched thoroughly. She went to Italy after a camping holiday in France, and visited Fiat, the factories, and the Gramsci Institute, where she picked up photographs of the period that were used in the production, a proof copy of Gramsci's *Prison Notebooks,* which had not then been published in England, and a copy of the Turin weekly paper *L'Ordine Nuovo (The New Order),* which the Communist leader and theoretician Gramsci had edited. It carried Romain Rolland's watchword, 'pessimism of the intellect, optimism of the will', and was reproduced with cast list and historical details as the production's newspaper-sized programme.

After a short tour, *Occupations* opened The Place season in October 1971. This arena production was the next step for Buzz Goodbody after *King John* in learning to work closely with a group of actors committed to a text, knowing they would share the exploration, and that their discoveries would be scrutinized under a microscope. The audience would be like the wallpaper of the hotel room where the action was mainly set, and in the factory scenes they would become the car workers. She brought her political understanding and approach to the rehearsals, putting into practice in a small company the ensemble philosophy of the RSC. There was a lot of discussion and exercises in political argument. A Communist gave a talk on Gramsci and the cast read background material. Inevitably, there were disagreements — the writer was a Socialist of one persuasion, the director a Communist, the actors and designer of different opinions — but the company, some of whom had come from *King John*, knit together, and the result was lucid, taut, exciting.

The production was well received, with praise going particularly to Ben Kingsley as Gramsci and Patrick Stewart as Kabak, the Bulgarian Communist and Comintern envoy, though many reviews had an air of surprise about them, as if to say 'I didn't know political drama could be so interesting'. Buzz Goodbody was disappointed at the response of some of the left press — from the *Seven Days* critic, who thought the play undermined its own possibilities by a romantic idolization of Gramsci, to the *Morning Star* reviewer, who said the absurdity of the arguments advanced by Kabak limited the play's general interest.

Though based on real events and people, including Kabak, *Occupations* was not an historical reconstruction, and certainly presented a one-sided view of Gramsci. It was an exploration of differing philosophies of political action, putting the question of why the workers' occupations had not led to a revolutionary movement. This was echoed in the clash between Gramsci and Kabak, between their views of political strategy and its relation to the individual, and in how they saw the masses. It was the first RSC production to affirm unambiguously a revolutionary commitment to socialism.

In form, however, there was no break with the RSC's previous 'political' drama. If anything, the production inside a single room was more 'naturalistic' — the factory meetings were simply played with the speeches amplified. Yet, while taking up one of the main themes from *King John* — the dilemma when knowledge confronts action — *Occupations* moved away from the showbiz side of that TGR production which had surfaced in her assistant's work in 1969, and was to appear again in *As You Like It* as a way of coping with the big stage. She was developing within an English radical tradition that springs from the non-conformists, making the characters real and believable, anchoring them in their social relationships as recognizable human beings. That meant a smooth-tongued but hard Fiat boss, not a monster in a top hat; it meant a beguiling, convincing Kabak, not a fatuous caricature of a cynical wheeler-dealer (which was how he was played in a television production of the play three years later). Buzz Goodbody had avoided the trap of a cut-price production, and had given respectability within the RSC to what was still seen as fringe activity, however important.

The season was boosted by three packed Sunday-evening performances of *The Oz Trial*, which brought the RSC back to the British political scene thanks to the 'fringe'. Buzz Goodbody had seen it in Bristol on a visit which turned out to be crucial for the future of the RSC. It had been written from the court papers by David Illingworth and Geoffrey Robertson, and directed as a late-night show at the Vic Studio by Howard Davies, who was to become artistic director of The Warehouse, bringing with him a group that had worked at Bristol and which helped to form the core of much of the RSC's new work. *The Oz Trial* was updated by the RSC as the appeal had just finished, and the show — an indictment of the obscenity laws — moved into the Aldwych for two late-night performances. The RSC was duly attacked for misusing public money.

The centrality of Shakespeare
Ironically, it was not modern work that really fired Buzz Goodbody. She felt that Shakespeare, coming between the Peasants' Revolt and the English Civil War, was as political in his way as any of her contemporaries — though she never posed one against the other. Neither, like some of her friends on the left, did she reject his work because it was a product of 'bourgeois culture' and irrelevant to the working class except to keep it in subjugation. Rather, she saw culture as important in the way ideas are formed, and so wanted to transform Shakespeare, and show how he explored his changing society in a concrete and complex way that could, therefore, be of value to ours. Shakespeare was, after all, the source to which innovators like Brecht or Bond returned time and again; he remains incomparably popular and influential in English-speaking culture; and he was what the RSC was all about. Challenging the traditions of Shakespeare production and reclaiming his plays for a modern audience offered a chance to put yourself in a new historical light, to redefine your attitudes within a continuity, and to help shift the emphasis and direction of those traditions.

Goodbody's preference for Shakespeare cast the mould for the distinctive contribution she and The Other Place made to the 1970s, though it was never in isolation from modern work. She had her chance to work on Shakespeare again when in 1972 Nunn asked her to be his assistant, with Euan Smith, on the most ambitious project since *The Wars of the Roses*. The *Romans* season — of *Coriolanus, Julius Caesar, Antony and Cleopatra,* and *Titus Andronicus* — was a debate about the issues behind the rise and fall of a society, and appropriate technical changes were made to the main theatre in Stratford; apart from the installation of a new lighting system, and minor changes to the seating, the stage was redesigned to thrust further into the auditorium and be more open. The gruelling experience of *The Romans* and its transfer to London, where Goodbody took more responsibility when Nunn fell ill, convinced her of Shakespeare's potential political relevance, especially as she worked a lot on the 'public' scenes. The citizens in *Coriolanus,* for example, were seen in their class context and given occupations, avoiding the proletarian heroes or mummerset cretins found in too many productions.

At that time, Goodbody was saying that the RSC should become more accountable to its audiences, less of an island, and more involved as an educational centre. Three *Romans* press showings in four days, seventeen weeks after the first production opened, convinced her that this was not the way to present Shakespeare, especially as the *Caesar* 'first night', like that of *John,* was a matinee, and the children spent more time chucking ice creams at each other than contemplating the wonder of political intrigue. But she learnt a great deal from working on a big stage with a big company, which was full of star names yet was trying to be an ensemble, and when she directed *As You Like It* at Stratford in 1973 she was convinced that she was working in the wrong space.

She tried approaching the male-female ambiguity of Rosalind from a feminist point of view, but all the research and explanations left most of the cast none the wiser. The leading man dropped out because of back strain, the leading woman tore a foot ligament as well as not getting on with Buzz Goodbody, and the pop appeal — maxi skirts and jeans against a tubular set — was sometimes at odds with her strong, mocking Chekhovian strain, exemplified in Richard Pasco's Jaques. The attempt, after the all-male National Theatre production of 1967, to win the play back for women did not work, though it had humanity, guts, and was fun. But Buzz Goodbody knew that she could not say what she wanted on the big stage, with actors using big-stage techniques. She was resorting to spectacle, to rhetoric, to pastiche, and that was not the answer: it only obscured and confirmed the mystique of the proscenium relationship between actor and audience. She knew she had to go somewhere else if she were to find her voice again, and the opportunity came with Nunn's invitation to her to become artistic director of The Other Place.

4. The first seasons at The Other Place

Buzz Goodbody's document on the second Stratford auditorium, dated December 1973, began with a realistic account of what resources the RSC had at the time, starting where Theatregoround left off with an artistic director, an administrative secretary or administrator, actors, directors, designers, and stage management on the RSC payroll (all with limited availability), and a building licensed for public performance with skeleton lighting and sound equipment. She said TGR 'started to go off the rails when as much money was spent on one show as the annual touring budget of the Freehold (a fringe group)', and stated at the outset a point of principle — that all projects should be mounted on a shoestring budget, which then meant £50 to £150 to cover everything.

Manifesto for a new theatre

Before considering the role of a second auditorium, she listed in six categories the uses to which the RSC then put studio work. It offered a chance for: i) junior or 'underparted' actors to get parts; ii) assistant directors (and others) to do things that interested them; iii) new plays to be performed by writers the RSC might be keen on; iv) greater experiment than was possible in the main auditorium; v) reaching a new audience as TGR had tried to do; and vi) serving the community. However, she noted that the two projects in the Stratford hut in 1973 (the Sylvia Plath and Ghelderode programmes) did not introduce new writers, did not seek a new audience, and did not serve the community. This 'do your own thing' policy belonged to internal not public work, although the second auditorium would have flexible enough planning to present publicly anything appropriate that emerged from it. The main point, nevertheless, was that any second-auditorium work should be aimed at the public, and that meant starting from 'practical as well as ideological' considerations. 'The RSC is financed by the whole of society', she claimed. 'We know why we play to an audience largely drawn from the upper and middle classes. We have to broaden that audience for artistic as well as social reasons. We know it'll take years. Unless we make the attempt — classical theatre will become like Glyndebourne'.

Her answer was to use to the best advantage what the RSC already possessed 'in terms of experience, interest, character and resources', and to match that to the possible audience for the second auditorium, which, she made quite clear, should not exist to fulfil the lives of the actors. This would be 'a side effect of its primary concern — its development of a wider audience for classical theatre'. Though the RSC did new or modern work, it was mainly a classical Shakespearian company, with actors who stayed, usually after a struggle 'up the ladder', because they wanted to act Shakespeare. They were not like actors who chose to work for 'fringe' groups such as 7:84, though later the 'fringe' companies were to provide many of the RSC's best new actors. Nor were the actors theatre-in-education experts or committed to communal/collective work methods in either the political or the physical sense, especially since Brook's departure.

But RSC actors did have knowledge and experience of complex classical texts and of paying attention to meaning as well as to entertaining. They did have an interest in more experimental writing, acting, and play presentation, if the latter was seen to be developing and not destroying their existing skills, and they were aware they had no links with their audiences. The strength of the RSC lay in the expert advice and talent of those who had stayed with the Company for several years, their experience of earlier schemes on the directing, acting, designing, and administrative side, and its resources in terms of property, costumes, and props, which exceeded those of any other theatre.

Buzz Goodbody made no bones about the problems facing her scheme when it came to audiences. Including Leamington and Warwick, but not Birmingham, in an imaginary circle that she had drawn around what she described as 'a sleepy Midlands market town that has come to be a shrine for international theatre', she saw hostile local and neighbouring communities. They were not, like Stoke and Newcastle, relatively well-established with an industrial working class, but tiny dormitory towns and villages for upper-class commuters in the centre of an agricultural region that had service industry, some labour-intensive horticulture nearby, and a mixture of landowners, farmers, and an industrial managerial stratum. But she also saw secondary school students — there were then fifteen schools within twenty miles — and the students at further education colleges, a polytechnic, an art school, and a university.

The largest potential audience, however, came from the visitors to Stratford, many of whom could not get tickets for the RST, but for various reasons stayed more than one day. She added that Coventry car workers were unlikely to make the journey because of the difficulty of getting back, that there was no real industrial, working-class cultural heritage locally to draw on, and no well-heeled, young professional audience to support the second auditorium as a 'fringe' venue. All roads led back to Shakespeare — as the mainstay. In the light of this, she listed seven types of project, each aimed at one or several categories of audience, and, although she felt that only a few of the projects could be presented, in the event four were included in the first season, two followed in the next, and only one still waits to be done — presenting a poem like *The Waste Land* as a play, in a project to be worked out with teachers.

The projects included in the first season were: a production of an exam text, planned with teachers, which turned out to be *Lear,* and the following year *Hamlet,* though the desired audience limit of 30 — presumably to make contact with the school students more productive — was never achieved; a documentary on the Shakespeare 'industry', which was written by John Downie with Penny Gold, and called *I Was Shakespeare's Double;* a history documentary for schools, *The World Turned Upside Down* by David Holman; and a new play, which, though Snoo Wilson is named in the document, was devised by Mike Leigh under the title *Babies Grow Old* (however, Wilson had a play performed by the RSC at The Place that year).

In the second season, two other projects were realized: a minor Elizabethan or Jacobean 'classic' — Ford's *Perkin Warbeck*, which replaced Goodbody's planned production of Jonson's *Epicene;* and Edward Bond's play about Shakespeare, *Bingo,* which she wanted to stage in Stratford for obvious reasons. The first season also included a revival of Rudkin's *Afore Night Come,* because of its local setting, as well as the important workshops, seminars, and discussions with the audience on Saturday mornings that have become one of the most popular of The Other Place's activities. There is one other scheme mentioned in the document that never got off the ground — a festival in high season, looking at classics, mainly Shakespearian, in a radically new way, using halls or gardens, or whatever spaces were available. Marowitz's *The Taming of the Shrew* and the Half Moon's *A Chaste Maid in Cheapside* by Middleton are mentioned as examples of the kind of work that might be undertaken.

Nunn read the document, and, with a few minor changes, it became the basis for the fight within the Company for the second Stratford auditorium. Buzz Goodbody addressed a planning committee on the basis of the document and the idea was given the go-ahead. She backed the name The Other Place, which was chosen from many suggestions — 'some absurd, some whimsical', remembers Nunn. It represented a continuation of the work at The Place, it implied a sense of the 'alternative', particularly in relation to the RST; it was suitably modest (there was a feeling that no one would remember its name); and, most important for Stratford, it was a quotation from Shakespeare (Hamlet telling Claudius where to find the dead Polonius).

The RSC finance committee recommended acceptance of the plan to the executive council, having taken the first decision of principle, especially in the face of Arts Council opposition, that The Other Place had to be 'self-financing'. This was later the case also with The Warehouse; and, very broadly speaking, self-financing they have been. What this means, again broadly speaking, is that two sums within the RSC's overall budget have to be done, to match what is wanted against available resources. Possible revenue (mainly from box office) is set against all the costs which arise only because the small theatre exists. The resources the RSC already has or needs — like actors, directors, designers, and production and administrative staff already on the payroll for a basic working week on rates fixed with the relevant unions, or materials already in the workshops, such as props left over from previous shows — are not counted. But pay for any staff engaged only on work for the small theatre, or overtime for anyone else if it is caused by the small theatre, or the costs of transport or of any material that has to be hired or bought just for a small-theatre production, or of publicity if it is not included in some other RSC publication or leaflet, has to be taken into account. Balancing the two figures before the productions start gives a target that is strictly and regularly 'policed' by the RSC's financial controller. Any 'loss' or 'gain' — terms relative only to the target figure — is absorbed within the RSC budget. If one show does well, that does not mean a bit extra can be passed on to another show. Likewise with commercial backing: a sum put up privately by a firm sponsoring one show is not counted as a 'saving' on that show's budget, and cannot be added to the budget of another.

Successes of the first season
Buzz Goodbody had asked for a female administrator, and the general manager suggested Jean Moore, who came back from a US tour of *The Dream* in January 1974 to take up the post. She had joined the RSC staff in 1966 in the Stratford box office and had moved across to TGR where she and Buzz Goodbody first met. They formed a tremendous partnership, and Jean Moore kept The Other Place style and discipline alive through the 1970s, giving the internal document to new members of staff to remind them of the theatre's origins. The first task the two tackled was to equip the building — the old dimmer board and three lanterns were hardly adequate. They bought dimmer racks, a 24-way board, which The Other Place still had in 1980, and second-hand lanterns, which they added to the lights left over from TGR, and they got hold of a sound console and tape deck from the tour of *The Dream*. All expenditure had to go through the general manager, but the watchword was to keep it as cheap as possible, and then cheaper still.

Later, when Buzz Goodbody wanted a permanent lighting operator, she asked Leo Leibovici, who had worked on the Roman plays at the Aldwych and on *Lear* in London, and who was to become as much a part of The Other Place team as anyone. All elements are heightened in the close confines of an intimate theatre working on a small budget but, with scenery at a minimum, lighting becomes crucial, taking on a special role in creating atmosphere and location. When Leibovici came to The Other Place, it had no rig: he stripped everything and started from scratch — his own empty space, which was in line with the philosophy of that second season as all shows were to be built up from an empty space, using flexible seating. He had to be able to light every part of the playing space with the available equipment, and soon learnt the necessary compromises and the limits of what he could and could not get away with — of how far into the audience he could light, for example, without them noticing or being blinded.

Leibovici designed a rig of two squares, and hung lights round them symmetrically, with the inner bar five feet higher than the outer, which hangs over the first row of the gallery and is within its reach. The lights, which can be plugged into any circuit, can be refocused between shows but not moved. The board is inadequate and the operators have to take risks: this means learning to reset quickly, as they can only set one cue ahead. The Other Place was painted black, the wooden flooring put in, and the RSC's carpenters built rough dressing-room work surfaces with mirrors where the TGR offices had been. The offices are still downstairs on the left as you go in through double doors from the car park, and alongside is a dressing room like a corridor that has stairs up to the gallery level. Upstairs is another dressing area divided into a larger and a smaller room, and on its right is the lighting and sound box. In front and to the sides is the gallery seating — wooden, with hard backs and folding seats, as below. Downstairs on the right are the toilets — though a Portaloo had to be used at first — and, beyond them, the auditorium, which then leads straight back to the outside world. The first seating units were painted by the actors and management with help from production staff. Buzz Goodbody and Jean Moore, who became a 'Jill of all trades', selling tickets, coke, and T-shirts from her office, painted the downstairs dressing room and the production controller painted the upstairs — a situation that, for obvious reasons of demarcation in less fluid circumstances, would be impossible in the years to come.

Goodbody and Moore met local teachers and drama advisers, and leafletted a wide area spreading as far as north Wales with details of the first production — a version of *King Lear,* a local exam text, specially shortened by Buzz Goodbody so that the school students could get back home after the show and the discussion which followed

— an idea prevalent on the 'fringe' for a time, though not new, but one which was dropped after this season. The main response from schools was that the RSC should come to them, which is what she did with *The World Turned Upside Down*. A different play from the one staged at the Cottesloe four years later, this was written by David Holman, who had worked for theatre-in-education teams, including the pioneering Coventry group, and looked at the English civil war locally in Warwickshire. Six actors, a musician, and a set of two screens, costumes, and props went off in a transit van to schools, where they put a screen at each end of a row of chairs — one was Van Dyck's triptych of Charles I, the other Glover's engraving of Parliament — and always stayed for a discussion after the play.

With secondary lighting and wiring fixed, The Other Place opened 'officially' on 10 April 1974. *Lear* was joined by the anti-establishment, mixed-media *I Was Shakespeare's Double,* directed by Howard Davies, a show that failed to please some of the governors once they got round to seeing it. The Stratford season was split in two that year, with a changeover half way through. In the second half, the quietly radical season was completed by *Babies Grow Old,* an improvised exploration of an elderly woman and her relatives, set on the outskirts of Birmingham; *The Tempest,* directed by Keith Hack, who had a reputation for excitement and originality; *Afore Night Come,* directed by Ron Daniels; and *Uncle Vanya,* 'starring' and directed by Nicol Williamson, who had just been in the play on Broadway. Davies, Hack, and Williamson were involved in RST productions, while Daniels and Leigh were freelance. Ironically, having been given her head to run the RSC's 'alternative' theatre, Goodbody was immediately landed with Williamson's production which had nothing to do with the ideology of the small theatre, and which seemed to be more a result of internal 'politics' — from which neither of the small theatres has ever been free.

Because of her treatment by the press, and her own experience of two press matinees, Goodbody did not invite the nationals to review *Lear,* which made more impact when it came to London. She also wanted to avoid the pressures that come from being on the national press circuit, when a lot, perhaps too much, is put into getting the show right for the critics, and success or failure tends to be judged by their standards and response. That has happened since, and contributes to the treadmill syndrome, which is also inherent in the company's tendency to measure success by expansion, fuelled by pressure from its funding sources and the needs of its artistic members.

The first leaflet about the new auditorium describes it as 'the RSC's small theatre in Stratford, seating 140. It is a conversion of the

Studio/Rehearsal space in Southern Lane'. In an internal newspaper, in a piece alongside an article by Barry Kyle who was running the rather literary season at The Place, Buzz Goodbody said: 'The Other Place is a first step towards ending the economic and social barrier between the RSC and the society that partly finances it. Its first aim is to offer good theatre cheaply — 60p for adults, 30p for kids. Its second aim is to work as members of a classical company in a small theatre where we can challenge our own traditions of proscenium theatre. Its third aim is to put on shows with a specifically local character, hopefully building an audience who hitherto thought the RSC were out of touch. Its fourth aim is to do specific educational projects for local schools, thus reaching out to a new younger audience. Its fifth aim is to create a forum where the audience can come into closer contact with the work of the company, for example, the free Saturday morning discussions and workshops'.

It had been an often lonely and frequently frustrating fight to get The Other Place off the ground, but Buzz Goodbody and those who backed her had done it. They had no reputation to worry about. They were excited and enthusiastic, and she threw parties. But many inside the company hardly knew it happened. The 'juniors-winning-spurs' feeling was still very strong, not to mention the idea which still persists that playing to 180 people (as the capacity later became) is a waste of time. For Nunn, however, it proved that Buzz Goodbody was becoming a fine classical director, that she could run The Other Place well, and that she could build a good team there. He saw that dovetailing did work and that, where possible, actors should be encouraged to work in both Stratford spaces.

Just after *Lear* opened in London, with two more shows to go at The Other Place, Buzz Goodbody wrote a memo — almost a full-time occupation in the RSC — reviewing the first season up to that point, and putting forward some proposals for the next. Without touching on the artistic merits of the productions (which, however, she said stood comparison with the best of TGR and 'in certain instances, with the work of our two big theatres'), she wrote that the 'new audience' policy had meant that 'we literally stepped out into the dark, never having run a small theatre in Stratford'. She continued: 'In a year when the RSC has done worse than usual in the big theatre in Stratford, The Other Place has done as follows: 1) *Lear* — sold out. 2) *I Was Shakespeare's Double* — sold out bar 1 performance. 3) *Babies Grow Old* — average of 40 per cent house. 4) *The Tempest* — on state of present bookings, sold out. 5) *The World Upside Down* — requested by three times as many schools as we can perform to'. She added that the Saturday morning sessions between June and August averaged 130 attendance. Her conclusion: 'The Other Place is obviously needed and not just by us. My firm conviction is that policy must be continued and enlarged next year. Before anyone screams, that doesn't necessarily mean more money'.

She made several technical and financial points — some of which had a bearing in the years following: the timing of openings in relation to main-house first nights, in order not to crowd the schedule of the production shops; getting more performances out of each piece of work — otherwise it is 'wasteful' and 'dispiriting', especially when some shows are only running for twelve performances; the need for a policy toward young designers; and keeping the budgets low (*Lear* £180, *Babies* £142, *World* £78), linked to careful planning to save money. She said that associates — the artists under flexible long-term contracts — not only should but must work at The Other Place, and added on casting, which had proved difficult in some cases, 'we run into grave problems if we ever field a second eleven'. Harking back to Hall's plan in the 1960s for a cheap-seat theatre at the Mercury in Notting Hill, West London, the base for Ballet Rambert, Goodbody went on: 'if we are committed to making classical theatre more accessible to the whole of society, the simple factor of cheap seats is most likely to produce the results we are after'.

Setting up the second season
Plans for the next season included Patrick Stewart and Sara Kestelman in *Antony and Cleopatra* (looking forward to Brook's treatment of it as a domestic play), to be performed as often as possible before exam time in front of schools audiences; a modern play, with *Bingo* still top of the list; and a new play to be scheduled in the high spot of summer to get the main-house overflow as well as the local audience. In addition to the Saturday-morning sessions, the 'poetry as drama' project was mentioned again; another documentary, which came to nothing, was mooted; and the idea of a high season 'fringe' festival, which never came off, was also floated.

Goodbody approached John Barton to direct *Antony* as the opening production of the second season, when the RSC returned to a full-year stretch. But he declined, and, following casting problems, it was dropped late for *Hamlet,* which shared some of the domestic preoccupations of *Antony* that were also present in *Lear*. There were plans, though, to revive the Nunn production of *Hamlet* at the RST with Alan Howard, who felt The Other Place production would stand in its way. A vote had to be taken on the planning committee, and The Other Place won.

After the first season's bad experiences with design (*The Tempest* and *I Was Shakespeare's Double*), Buzz Goodbody asked Howard

41

Davies to suggest someone who could work on three shows to give continuity, and he brought in Chris Dyer for *Hamlet, Epicene* (to be directed by Buzz Goodbody as the 'minor classic'), and Brecht's *Man is Man,* which Davies was to direct himself. Dyer, who had been a scene painter for five years at the Bristol Old Vic after studying at art school, was to design over a dozen shows for the two small spaces between 1975 and 1979, and became the RSC's resident designer in 1978, in charge of the permanent staging at Stratford and at the Aldwych.

Buzz Goodbody came back from the US, where *Lear* was touring, to rehearse *Hamlet,* which opened on 8 April 1975, although the official first night was not until 15 May. The national critics were invited this time, partly because freelance directors like Ron Daniels the season before had insisted, as their livelihood depended on it, and partly because the threat of closure always hung over The Other Place — the RSC crisis came to a head in 1975 — and 'success' was a lever against that. Interest had also been kindled by the first season, particularly by *Lear,* which transferred to The Place, *Afore Night Come,* which seemed prophetic, and *Babies Grow Old,* which did well in a London 'fringe' venue, the ICA, in 1975. On 12 April, Buzz Goodbody was found dead in the north London house where she lived, with empty pill boxes, a note, and Eliot's *The Four Quartets* by her bed. Trevor Nunn was in Los Angeles on the *Hedda Gabler* tour, and came back to take *Hamlet* through its run and its all-too-short transfer to the Roundhouse Downstairs in 1976, alongside *Man is Man,* with Brook's *The Ik* from Paris in the main auditorium.

Barry Kyle took over The Other Place for the rest of the season, bringing in an entertainment about words, *The Mouth Organ,* dismantling *Epicene,* as was only right, and replacing it with *Perkin Warbeck,* which he and John Barton directed with not enough time, lots of props, and twelve musicians on a cumbersome set. It was a 'main-house' affair crammed into The Other Place, and much the same could be said of *Richard III.* At the end of the season there was another discussion about the future of The Other Place, and another memo, this time from Barry Kyle, who was not keen to continue as artistic director, Jean Moore, Leo Leibovici, and Andrew Tansley on the production side. They said a decision had to be taken over the space. Buzz Goodbody and Chris Dyer had wanted an open-space season in 1975 at £230 a show, but this had caused technical problems, like closing the theatre during the day while all the staff changed the seating for the next night's show. Sets only took ten minutes to shift. No rehearsals could take place there, which meant hiring other spaces, and that meant adding to the budget.

If a permanent auditorium were to be built to overcome this problem, the memo continued, its design would have to be agreed in advance by all concerned, and it would mean the end of the 'empty space' notion. However, if that were to be kept going, the RSC would have to drop its repertoire system — which had no particular advantage for Other Place audiences, and several disadvantages. Shows were out of the programme for a week or more, which affected their durability; there were lots of time-consuming line runs; and it could be hit or miss for the public as to whether or not they were able to see a particular production — all running counter to the idea of repertoire, which is supposed to allow productions to mature over a period of time. It also threw up terrible storage problems (at first, storage was in a lorry parked outside, but in 1978 a Nissen hut was built for The Other Place, alongside the two wardrobe hire huts that stand in a row with the theatre).

The Kyle memo therefore argued for straight runs, which, it was claimed, worked well at the end of 1974. Already aware of the pre-booking sell-out problem, which took away the need for a good review to fill the seats, the memo suggested staggered press nights, with critics coming whenever they wanted. This would also relieve actors from the strain of what was then a second-night press show, and the associated paranoia and rush. The memo pressed for a programme that was varied in spirit and content, which did not include prestige or pet projects designed to meet a whim or a casting trade-off, and for cast size to be restricted to eleven. The decision went against straight runs, with exceptions like *The Alchemist* which had a difficult set to move; the cast-size limitation was ignored; and a permanent auditorium was designed by Chris Dyer, John Napier, and Dermot Harris for the 1976 season under Trevor Nunn. The new seating arrangement was four-sided, with a maximum capacity of 180. Plays could be staged in the round or, which was more often the case, on three sides, with the possibility of using the fourth side as a gallery acting area.

The continuing role of The Other Place

Nunn had been deeply influenced by Buzz Goodbody and her death, not only as head of the Company but as a close friend. It was no accident that he himself decided to take over the running of The Other Place, and it was there that he knew he would come to grips with *Macbeth,* which he had already directed in 1974 and 1975 on large stages. For Nunn, 1976 was to be 'the most enjoyable year of my life at the RSC'. He chose the plays, the casts, the designers, and directors, achieving a co-ordination with the RST productions that he had aimed at in the last two years of TGR. The season was a watershed for the RSC's other space, which had established itself through success in London — with *Lear* and *Babies Grow Old* from the first season, and *Man is Man* and (most influentially) *Hamlet* from the second. Now the Company's chief executive and artistic director was at the helm, and one of Britain's leading actors, Ian McKellen, would only play Leontes and Romeo on the big stage if he could act at The Other Place as well. The productions, all very well received, were: *Schweyk* and *Bingo,* directed by Howard Davies; *Dingo* directed by Barry Kyle; Nunn's *Macbeth*, with McKellen and Judi Dench, which also played at the RST; and one of the most important plays of the 1970s, David Edgar's anti-fascist *Destiny,* directed by Ron Daniels, which transferred to the Aldwych. Like *Macbeth, Destiny* was also televised — quite a double coup for The Other Place.

Whereas at first people had to cadge and cajole to get help on productions at The Other Place, it was now on the RSC's schedules, whether you were in wigs, wardrobe, or the workshops. But, at the same time, there was little stress on the community side, and the educational impetus had gone. Guided by Nunn, a group of actors had emerged under the influence of Davies, Daniels, Kyle, and a new casting director, Joyce Nettles, that was committed to The Other Place. Most had come from the 'fringe' and some — for the first time in the Company's history — were doing more work at the smaller theatre than the large. This core of actors and the style they developed contributed more to the continuity of The Other Place, and later The Warehouse, than even the directors and designers, and together they gave an identity to the smaller theatres that was missing from the main houses.

Nunn chose Ron Daniels to follow him as artistic director of The Other Place in December 1976. Daniels was going from strength to strength, with *Afore Night Come* and *Destiny* already to his credit, and his background in the theatre gave him the right kind of experience. He was born and bred in Brazil of English parents, and while remaining an outsider, identified with his environment. With half a dozen Brazilian friends, he helped to build — literally — the Theatre Workshop, called Officino, in Sao Paulo, which was part of the political and social upsurge in that country cut short by the military coup in 1964. Isolated from many developments in the theatre, this group read about Brecht, the European experiments of Brook, Strehler in Italy, Planchon in France, and wanted to go to Europe to study. Daniels came to England on a drama scholarship, and acted with Peter Cheeseman's influential Stoke company, with which he worked on and off from 1965 to 1971. He came to the RSC in 1968 to act in *Merry Wives,* when he met Buzz Goodbody, and discovered that he did not want to be an actor.

He went back to Stoke, and directed a range of plays from a Greek double bill through *Hamlet* to *Major Barbara,* and then worked a lot on the 'fringe', directing Steve Gooch's *Female Transport* at the Half Moon (1973), Gooch and Paul Thompson's *The Motor Show* (1974), about Ford, at Dagenham, the corporation's home, and later at the Half Moon, and another Gooch and Thompson play about the car industry, *Made in Britain*, at Oxford (1976). Daniels has also directed for television, in the US, and for the National Youth Theatre. It was while he was directing Thompson's *By Common Consent* for the professional wing of the National Youth Theatre that Buzz Goodbody asked him, via Rudkin's agent, to direct *Afore Night Come*. He refused to be an assistant at the RSC and did the production as a freelance. He was to have directed Rudkin's *Ashes* when it was first staged at the Open Space, but he and Charles Marowitz disagreed — though he did direct it in 1975 at the Young Vic. It was Daniels who approached Nunn with *Destiny*, which, Nunn says, 'we were lucky to get, we didn't deserve it', having already joined the long list of theatres which initially rejected the play.

When Daniels became artistic director of The Other Place he was given no brief, except that the theatre had to pay its way. There was no democratic structure introduced to run the theatre, which like the rest of the RSC, including The Warehouse, operates under a system of pressures, influence, trust, and delegation. Daniels, who became an associate of the RSC in 1979, says he has avoided the burden of committee work, and deals 'up the ladder' only with Nunn, Hands, or the financial controller. His choice of plays has also been pragmatic, matching many requirements to certain preferences, starting with plays he would like to direct himself. He has a special relationship with writers like Rudkin and Thompson, with whom he often works on scripts, and a liking for an epic approach that places the individual in great detail against a social and political background rather than indoors. This, he says, might stem from spending his boyhood in cinemas and not theatres, watching movies by people like John Ford and Eisenstein. Daniels talks of plays that look at 'how we face and make choices' and at 'the desire to change and the pressure to conform' — themes that run through the RSC's small-scale work of the 1970s from *King John* onwards.

If he cannot himself direct a play he has chosen, Daniels will see whether anyone else is willing or able to do so, and will also look at plays he thinks deserve to be done. Suggestions come in from others like Howard Davies or Walter Donohue, nominally the literary manager for The Other Place as well as The Warehouse. Daniels says The Other Place cannot do the 'urban' plays that have become a hallmark of The Warehouse, but thinks that his policy of giving playwrights a second or third production of a play that might otherwise not be produced for reasons of taste, box office, or resources — such as *The Churchill Play* or *Dingo* — is as important a service to writers as is The Warehouse policy of staging their new work. In this vein, Daniels has also established The Other Place as a theatre that 'reclaims' the classics, carrying on from the Shakespeare work of Goodbody and Nunn with productions like Barton's *The Merchant of Venice,* or in new versions of classics, like Rudkin's *Hippolytus* or Thompson's *Lorenzaccio Story.*

There are practical considerations, like going for large-cast plays, which, despite the cramped conditions, Daniels thinks vital in view of the size of the RSC, both to keep as many actors occupied as much as possible, and because it is what the RSC can offer that other theatres cannot. Most important, he says, is judging the venue and what the audience wants — like Shakespeare, as he discovered the year he left him out. The Other Place is not the Half Moon. Equally, it is not full of rich tourists or stockbrokers, but a cross-section of the English-speaking middle class. Daniels is the first to admit that a manual working-class audience would not put up with the conditions.

Since Buzz Goodbody's document, there has been no attempt by any of the subsequent artistic directors to define or analyze policy in the same detail. Nevertheless, a pattern emerges — which has to be seen in relation to the development of the rest of the RSC, in particular The Warehouse. This shows a move away from the Goodbody principles toward a situation from which she was trying to escape. Stratford remains an international theatre shrine — but with two theatres, and a more mixed programme. By the 1979 season (*Pericles, Baal, The Suicide, Anna Christie,* and *The Three Sisters*), The Other Place had moved away from educational or community work, and for the first time did not present a new play .(though Erdman's *The Suicide,* written and banned in 1932 in the Soviet Union, had not been seen on the stage in Britain before). The Other Place was starting to become its own 'establishment', with its own style of highly polished (and highly successful) cosmopolitan theatre — reminiscent of a previous RSC era, albeit an exciting one, but lacking risk and surprise. There seemed no space to experiment with new styles of performance or staging, a feature that was also missing from the rest of the theatre scene. However, by the end of the 1979 season, The Other Place had notched up a remarkable record: seven Shakespeares, three plays by his contemporaries, three Brechts, seven new plays, five revivals of plays by living authors, two Chekhovs, one O'Neill, one Soviet play, one 'documentary', one compilation show, and two local tours. Five shows had transferred to larger auditoria, two had been televised, and one, *Piaf,* had gone into the West End. The Other Place had become as much a part of Stratford for the theatregoer as the Royal Shakespeare Theatre itself.

5. The opening of The Warehouse

The opening of The Warehouse sounds like one of those myths that the insecure theatre profession is so fond of producing — everyone pulling together not just to get the shows on, but to get the theatre open in time. With the RSC locked into its two-year Stratford-London operation, and The Other Place well established with a core of actors committed to its work, there was an overriding argument — practical, artistic, and ideological — in favour of a permanent second auditorium in the capital. This was reinforced by the first RSC visit to Newcastle, when, in March 1977, it took four productions from the RST to the Theatre Royal and four from The Other Place to the 160-seat Gulbenkian Studio in the University Theatre. During the five-week season, there were also 'special' RSC activities in other theatres and arts centres, from 'open theatre days' and schools workshops to lunchtime and late-night entertainments, anthology performances, and after-show discussions.

A theatre for new British plays

Nunn, with his ear characteristically tuned in to the rising generation, had asked Howard Davies to run with him, for one year at least, the new London theatre. Davies, once a stage manager after studying on a directors' course at Bristol University, had been artistic director of the Bristol Old Vic Studio, where his credits included *Narrow Road to the Deep North, Early Morning, Long Day's Journey into Night, Endgame, Troilus and Cressida,* and *Fears and Miseries of the Third Reich.* He also adapted with Bill Alexander two children's shows and co-directed with him two plays of local interest, David Edgar's *The Case of the Workers' Plane,* which tells the story of the Bristol aerospace industry and in particular the argument over Concorde, and David Illingworth's *The Bristol Ring-Road Show.* Davies directed several shows for the Bristol 'fringe' group Avon Touring, which friends of his had set up in 1974, and as a freelance he directed *The Threepenny Opera, The Caucasian Chalk Circle,* and *Afore Night Come.* In 1975 he directed *Bevan: Struggles against the Iron Hell* for the Welsh Drama Company: this was the story of 40 years of labour history by his close friend David Illingworth (who died of cancer the following year).

Davies had first worked with the RSC in 1974 as a result of Buzz Goodbody's trip to Bristol to see his production of *The Oz Trial.* He had mistrusted the RSC's 'Cambridge clique', who always seemed to be quoting Shakespeare to each other, and had turned down an offer from Barton. It was only a conversation with Buzz Goodbody that changed Davies's mind, and he helped Barton on *King John*, as well as directing *I Was Shakespeare's Double* at The Other Place and Snoo Wilson's *The Beast* at The Place — both of which he thought he had messed up. When he was asked back for the second season at The Other Place, he chose and cast Brecht's *Happy End,* but was beaten to it by the Oxford Playhouse. Davies switched to *Man is Man* after RSC literary manager Ronald Bryden suggested he tried Steve Gooch's version, which had been used by the Royal Court, and 'it clicked'.

This production was paired with *Hamlet* in the Roundhouse season, which linked Davies publicly to The Other Place and its philosophy. The identification was strengthened when Nunn asked him to work a third time there, directing not just another Brecht — *Schweyk in the Second World War* — but the play Buzz Goodbody had always wanted to stage, Edward Bond's *Bingo*. In between these two, Davies directed *The Iceman Cometh* at the Aldwych. It was during the rehearsals for the O'Neill play that Nunn approached Davies to become an RSC associate director — which, apart from the early case of Michel Saint-Denis, was unprecedented for someone who had not directed Shakespeare with the Company and did not want to. There was a gap of many months before anything was agreed. Davies remembered his talk with Buzz Goodbody about fighting within the organization for what one wanted, yet this turned out to be what Nunn had already decided the RSC needed — a theatre presenting new British plays.

Still suspicious of the RSC, Davies discussed the possibilities with friends and colleagues, including Edward Bond, who said it would be worth doing if it meant creating an outlet for new writing, and promised to write a play to help. Davies said 'yes' to the RSC on condition that his work 'accommodated my background and experience', and was at first taken on to supervise scripts. Neither he nor Nunn could run the new theatre on their own: Nunn was too busy and 'out of touch', Davies too inexperienced. Although Buzz Goodbody had paved the way with The Other Place, there was resistance within the Company at the top levels as well as from the Arts Council, and all the arguments had to be won again, especially as to 'pay your way' was harder in London than Stratford. Thus, the RSC paid no rent for The Other Place but would have to for the new theatre; the minimum conversion work and basic equipment would be costly, and sets would have to be built on contract because the RSC workshops were in Stratford; and overheads would be much higher, while the Company would be getting less and less for its money as time went on and inflation bit deeper.

The first season's programme had to be planned and rehearsals started before a suitable building had been found. As at The Other Place, shows would run in repertory, cast 'back-to-back' with main-house productions, but the new London theatre would have a distinctive policy of staging new British plays alongside Other Place transfers. This would offer economic security, as well as a chance for The Other Place work to be seen in the capital.

In choosing the opening plays, the first task was to sort through a nine-month backlog of some 200 scripts, in which Davies was helped by a 'panel' of Nunn, Jones, Williams, Kyle, and Daniels. The influential 'fringe' director Chris Parr sent in *That Good Between Us*, by Howard Barker, and this was chosen as the official opening production — on 28 July 1977 — against opposition which was pushing for *Macbeth* as a safe box office bet (an example of the kind of tension that has beset the relationship between The Warehouse and other parts of the RSC ever since). The National Theatre, which has a habit of 'buying' lots of scripts but staging very few, had had an option on Barker's play but agreed to release it to the RSC. Davies, however, lost *Once a Catholic* to the Royal Court, though he did commission Mary O'Malley to write another comedy for The Warehouse. C. P. Taylor's *Bandits* also landed on Davies's desk, and the subject interested him. With Illingworth, he had researched the 'mafia' of the North East as another side of the 'swinging sixties' of dope-smoking students, and he was keen on promoting writers who were not based in London. Additionally, the RSC had just returned from its trip to Newcastle upon Tyne, where the play was set, where Taylor lived — and where the first production of the play, by a community group, 'On the Side', had been given.

James Robson's *Factory Birds*, which won the *Evening Standard*'s Best New Play award, had been turned down by the Birmingham Rep, and came to the RSC's notice through a Bristol colleague of Davies's, Walter Donohue, who was helping read scripts and was later to become literary manager for The Warehouse. Donohue had worked with Peter Gill, who had directed Robson's first play on television, while Jon Amiel, who assisted Davies on *The Days of the Commune* at the Aldwych, had directed Robson's *Forgive Me Delilah* at the Soho Poly. There was Bond's promised play, which turned out to be *The Bundle,* and to finish the season Davies wanted a more relaxed, 'popular' piece. He approached Barrie Keeffe after seeing *Gimme Shelter* when it transferred from the Soho Poly to the Royal Court, and the result was *Frozen Assets*. Steve Gooch's *How the Peace was Lost* was scheduled, but was dropped for a number of internal reasons to do with the cast and the fact that Daniels had won his long battle to get Gooch's *Women Pirates* put on at the Aldwych. Another clash had meant Davies putting off Pam Gems's *Piaf* until her *Queen Christina* had finished its Stratford run, and he accordingly directed *Piaf* at The Other Place in the following season.

Adapting the space

Davies lost one-and-a-half stone getting the first season on, and the new theatre open. Whereas The Other Place had grown slowly and modestly (and in a building already owned by the Company), the RSC had had to go out and find its second London theatre — no easy matter in an unstable speculators' market — and to open it more abruptly. The Place, which had been used in 1971, 1973, and 1974, was unavailable, and the Roundhouse, which had last been used in 1976, was unsuitable; in any case, the Company's needs had gone beyond what either of those venues could have offered or coped with. The logistics of the RSC operation called for a theatre under RSC control and preferably one near to the Aldwych and to the Covent Garden rehearsal rooms.

Months of footslogging by the management around dingy, deserted dance halls and damp basements led them to Poupart's Warehouse in the desired location, Covent Garden. But three months before its opening, the RSC had to change plans as fire regulations would have meant buying the two shops on either side and building corridors through them to the theatre. Luckily, however, the Donmar Theatre opposite was available, and, though by no means perfect, was the only chance left. Built in the 1870s as a vat room for a big brewery, it was sold in the 1920s to a film company and became the first studio in Britain to use colour. The fruit trade took it over as a warehouse for banana-ripening until 1960, when theatre manager Donald Albery bought it, foreshadowing the future of Covent Garden as an arts centre instead of a market. He named it Donmar after himself and Margot Fonteyn, and it was often used for ballet because of its size and its mirrors. The RSC had staged scenes from *The Screens* as part of its *Theatre of Cruelty* season there in 1964, and was using it for rehearsals before taking over permanent rehearsal space round the corner in Floral Street.

The hard work began to convert it into a theatre conforming to the strict London regulations for live performance, while also keeping it available to take productions transferred from The Other Place. The minimum conversion work required to meet even the occasional performing licence (granted just for the opening) was a big minimum, and every RSC department had to cut back to get the theatre open. But they did it — helped by having Nunn not only completely behind the project, but also as its main driving force within the Company. On top of obvious matters like wiring and plumbing, the main problem was access: the auditorium was not at street level and the RSC had to build exits, one of which, at the back, had to be carved out as none existed. The first show to be staged there — *Schweyk,* though this was not the official opening production — started half-an-hour late because the electricity had been turned on only half-an-hour before the scheduled beginning, and the concrete steps, which had to be rebuilt as they had fallen two feet short, had still not set.

It is not easy to find the building nor even the way in, but when you have, you enter under a discreet sign and make your way along a cold concrete-and-brick corridor, made cheerier by the addition of production photographs, up and round a stairbend, past toilets, and into a small area where there is a bookstall (completing the utilitarian atmosphere with foolscap, cyclostyled programmes), and where at half-time the staff sell soft drinks and ice creams (for alcohol there's a pub down the road, now equipped with its own warning bell). You can sit anywhere in The Warehouse, but there is no escaping the uncomfortable plastic, orange cafeteria seats, whether upstairs in the gallery or on the same level as the acting area. The high-ceilinged auditorium, which seats a maximum of 200 on three sides, was designed to take productions from the Newcastle Gulbenkian Studio, which partly explains the poor sightlines it shares with that theatre. Beyond the auditorium, with its bare floorboards and brick wall at the back, there is another corridor out to the street. Off this are the cramped, partitioned dressing rooms and the offices — two were built 'in the air' with a music store out of recycled wood.

When The Warehouse had to change to a full performing licence, the RSC had to clear up the backstage chaos and build a scenery and props cupboard next to the lighting and sound boards, on the right and above as you enter the auditorium. This can make access and production changeovers difficult. Everything not being used in the show about to be performed has to be kept in one of the docks, though the RSC's 'modern' wardrobe store is in the Floral Street rehearsal rooms. Unlike The Other Place, which works on a village-hall licence, The Warehouse has to use material that is inherently flameproof, not just fireproofed, and this bumps up the cost.

The Warehouse also has better lighting boards and lanterns because all the old stock was used up to equip The Other Place. The London theatre is more spacious than the Stratford space, and is less rough — though nothing like the purpose-built, black auditorium of the National's small-space theatre, the Cottesloe, which has budgets anything from two to six times greater than its RSC counterpart across the river. In Stratford, you have the fresh, open air outside, the church bells, and bowling green, and everyone has to wait together in the car park in rain, snow, frost, or sun with no pub to escape to. In London, there is a feeling of being inside a box inside another box, which might be just another isolated building in an unfriendly metropolis.

The first season at The Warehouse put it on the map, however. The productions were a success, artistically and with the public, and were performed by one of the strongest companies the RSC had formed in the 1970s. When many other theatres were flagging, and new writing was having a hard time, the opening of The Warehouse was an act of faith in the social role of drama — however marginal it may have seemed given the small capacity of the auditorium. Here was a mark of the vigour that had come from the 'fringe', and of the ability of a major subsidized company to debate crucial issues and be provocative at a time when a political turn to the right was accompanied by increased economic instability. It was appropriate that this new examination of ourselves and our society was taking place in a warehouse — symbol of a nation's true wealth created by labour.

Control and constraints

In the media, every effort was being made to promote an intellectually bankrupt but ever more powerful right-wing intelligentsia as the new voice of reason, common sense, and order (the contrast was underlined when The Warehouse presented in early 1979 a season of 'plays television would not do', by Trevor Griffiths, Howard Barker, Roy Minton, Steve Gooch, Snoo Wilson, Stephen Lowe, and Trevor Preston. Politics, mainly, and sex, were the sticking points, though the readings and discussions picked up other controversies, like television's antagonism to anything non-naturalistic.) Since the opening of The Warehouse, Howard Davies has tried to build a team to help give shape to its policy — which has remained artistically narrow, despite ranging in verbal style from the taut, ferocious language of Barker to the more affectionate prose of Mary O'Malley. This young group, each of whose members has directed at the theatre, was not a collective, nor did it include any technical staff, actors, designers, or writers. It comprised Howard Davies as artistic director, Walter Donohue as head of the literary department, Bill Alexander, John Caird, and Barry Kyle.

American-born, Donohue came to Bristol University as a postgraduate in 1967. He worked as Charles Marowitz's assistant at the Open Space, went back to Bristol when Davies was running the Vic Studio, and directed there work by Brenton, Genet, Arrabal, and Shepard. He directed Paul Foster's *Queen Elizabeth* at the Royal Court Theatre Upstairs; *The Can Opener* for the RSC at The Place (on Davies's suggestion); three shows, including *Occupations*, at The Space, Capetown; worked with Peter Gill on *As You Like It, The Fool,* and *The Recruiting Officer;* and on two projects at the National. As literary manager, Donohue was the main contact between The Warehouse and the writers, and was in charge of the scripts that came in, which he and a team of readers assessed. He also initiated projects, like the late-night production *A Miserable and Lonely Death,* based on the inquest into the killing of Black Consciousness leader Steve Biko (the proceeds of the show went to the International Defence and Aid Fund). Other projects have included play-readings, The Warehouse Writers series of notes on plays that are being performed and their authors, publishing plays and poems by playwrights, and helping to set up a new writers scheme with the Gulbenkian Foundation.

Bill Alexander had joined the RSC in 1977 as an assistant director to Barton on *The Way of the World,* and to Nunn on *The Alchemist* at The Other Place and *King Lear* at the RST. He became a resident director, a new post, in 1978, attached to The Warehouse. Previously, Alexander had worked with Inter-Action, at the Bristol Old Vic (co-directing with Davies *The Case of the Workers' Plane* and *The Bristol Ring-Road Show,* and adapting with him two children's shows), at the Royal Court (where he directed, among other plays, *Class Enemy* by Nigel Williams), and as a freelance at Nottingham, Newcastle, and elsewhere. John Caird also joined the RSC in 1977 as an assistant — to Nunn on *As You Like It* at the RST, and to Daniels on *Lorenzaccio* and *'Tis Pity* at The Other Place. Like Alexander, he became a resident director, having worked as a freelance on the 'fringe' in Manchester with Contact Theatre, in Bristol with Avon Touring, and in London with Sidewalk Theatre. 'Senior' RSC director of the team, Barry Kyle became an associate of the Company in 1979, and ran The Other Place briefly after Buzz Goodbody's death. He first joined in 1973 as an assistant after working at the Liverpool Playhouse, where he was in charge of workshop projects and the schools programme.

The team never worked in a formal way, but acted more as a means of swopping ideas. The imprint on policy, however, was firmly, but not exclusively, that of Davies. But after planning the first season, his workload spread, as is often the case, and the programme went adrift — partly due to poor judgement, and partly to reasons beyond the control of The Warehouse team, like late delivery of commissioned scripts, or the adverse effect of a bad Aldwych box office.

Like The Other Place, The Warehouse has to operate within the RSC system, benefiting from and existing because of its advantages, while suffering from its disadvantages. The Warehouse policy of commissioning and staging new plays by British writers looks simple enough, but is much more difficult in practice. Putting on new writing should not be an issue, especially in Britain, yet it is — and the mixed economy is not the most favourable for fostering it. Although the publicly-subsidized sector has been indispensable to the flowering of new work, the scale and range of which would never have been possible under a private commercial system, it has had to operate within the limits of shamefully inadequate funding. The amounts allocated are derisorily low, the timing and period of guarantee make long-term planning a gamble, and too much of the decision-making takes place in secret. Since the war, there has only been a brief economic 'breathing space' for the RSC, and the achievements of that period in the late 1960s and early 1970s were hard won.

In the RSC, the allocation of resources is subject to a series of negotiations, over many of which the artistic director of The Warehouse has little or precarious control — and the writer almost none. At any moment in a Company of that size there will be a crisis, and the more serious it is the more it is likely to be resolved in favour of the 'main' theatres, because that is where the money comes in. Thus, an unofficial and largely unspoken ranking order emerges within the RSC: first the RST in Stratford, then the Aldwych, then The Other Place, and last The Warehouse, which has all the problems associated with a location in central London, as well as having a bigger programme than its Stratford counterpart, and the difficulties of presenting new work. Life in the RSC begins in Stratford and then travels to London. Innovation, however, usually travels in the other direction. Moreover, productions from the smaller spaces have filled main house slots — *Macbeth, Destiny, The Alchemist, The Dance of Death,* and *Piaf* — and have kept the RSC in the public eye, thereby helping to put the all-important 'bums on seats'.

Problems of presenting new work

For all the problems, the RSC is able to offer at The Warehouse resources that any 'fringe' theatre would give its eye teeth for — not to mention the 'advantage' of greater publicity, more critical attention, and a better chance to be published or taken up by television. Even without the Stratford workshops, The Warehouse still draws on an outstanding back-up team of voice teachers under Cicely Berry, fight arrangers, dance instructors such as Gillian Lynne, technical and administrative staff, as well as designers, directors, and actors, all of a high standard across the board. Many actors would not work with the RSC if it were not for the two small theatres. Casting for any season takes the larger and the smaller theatres into equal account, and only the National could consistently offer the size of cast to new writers that can be found in The Warehouse. Thus, while economics has played its part in forcing the 'fringe' to look 'inward' to more interior plays with smaller casts, The Warehouse, like The Other Place, has almost always staged broad, public works.

Casting is very important for new plays, not just because their identity is being created for the first time, but also because many exploit the intimacy of the space with the eye of a television camera, using naturalism to produce a 'slice of life'. Consider a majority sampling of the plays presented at The Warehouse in its first four seasons: *Bandits, Factory Birds, Frozen Assets, Savage Amusement, A and R, Shout Across the River, Look Out . . . Here Comes Trouble, The Innocent,* and *Men's Beano.* With all their differences, the common denominator is clear — as is the vulnerability to the pressures of the RSC operation. The 'naturalistic', understated, unrhetorical style of such work ran counter to the approach that established the RSC as a notable acting company of Shakespeare on its main stages. The small spaces threw up a new style that contested the stand-and-deliver approach, but often only as its opposite, as was seen in the 1978-79 RST seasons — for example, Bob Peck's blunt Iago to Donald Sinden's florid Othello.

Despite a noticeable decline in the verse speaking on the main stages, which has a lot to do with the influence of the small spaces, the new writers who use language in a distinctive, literary way, like Brenton, Barker, or Rudkin, have benefited enormously from having their work presented by the RSC. On the other hand, regional writers like Taylor and Tom McGrath, who pose problems of accent, have suffered. But when it comes to a play like *The Bundle,* although the RSC actors' grasp of language was invaluable, the problem went beyond being the right height or weight, or coping with an accent. Bond questioned the basis of the actors' craft. There was no character, only social determinants in a process of change. In the circumstances, Howard Davies's production of *The Bundle* was remarkable, especially as it fell at the end of a testing season.

Actors who were fed up with the hierarchical, commercial system, and the parts it offered, were an important force in the rise of the 'studio' movement. The new spaces excited them even more than they did most directors. In the beginning on the 'fringe', there was commitment to new ideas but not always the techniques effectively to present them. Energy and the occasion are often enough, though political differences can be every bit as divisive, if not more so, than anything seen in the RSC. But the stakes are different, and there are important points of contradiction in the RSC cross-fertilization process. An actor develops the commitment and skills required to present Shakespeare as truthful to our times. An actor also develops the commitment and skills required to present contemporary writers who are as true to their times as Shakespeare was to his. But 350 years separates the two Elizabethan ages.

Along with plays by Edgar, Barker, and Brenton, *The Bundle* thus put its finger on the problem of the professional ethic. An actor has to be truthful in the close-up conditions of the small theatres, and, therefore, has to be convinced of the part and of the role it has in the play. At what point does the ideology clash with the deployment of skills? Actors walked out of *Frozen Assets,* which contains attacks on upper-class attitudes and behaviour; and actors in *Queen Christina,* who did not understand the play, proved difficult to the director because of their opposition. Such contradictions have thrown up the need for a new aesthetic, but how capable is the theatre of creating it?

At least the style of presentation in the small spaces has kept in step with a questioning section of society, and with the plays that spoke for it. But for The Warehouse this is the first, and most basic, area over which the artistic director has no control. Half the shows have been chosen by someone else in Stratford. There *is* continuity, however, from the actors and designers, and The Warehouse team does work at The Other Place and make suggestions about its programme. In the first season at The Warehouse, for example, Davies had directed two of the transfers. Different ways have been tried of slotting the transfers into the London repertoire — the most successful artistically being to alternate them, one Stratford, one new play, and so on (this has also made the new work less vulnerable to the ups and downs of the Aldwych box office), though RSC financial considerations led to the 1980 transfers being played *en bloc,* to pay off a huge deficit.

But Stratford 'hits' bring problems as well as security. Many of them, particularly the Shakespeares, are sold out in advance through the RSC mailing list. If, then, the Brenton addict decides to change the habit of a lifetime and try the Bard, as the cross-fertilization philosophy would have it, the door is often shut. This makes it difficult for The Warehouse to build the active relationship with its audience which every theatre needs. And this is especially true in London, in the face of intense cultural competition, with its stress on radical chic, and the 'supermarket' pressure of 'new equals good'. The Warehouse has a hard enough time as it is, with its less than welcoming front-of-house space that cannot cope with people even if they do stray in, its lack of any relationship with the lively Covent Garden community, and the absence of posters proclaiming the theatre's presence in one of the most intensely fly-posted areas of London. It is also difficult when you have to buy your tickets ten minutes walk away at the Aldwych because there is neither enough room for a box office nor enough money to staff one at The Warehouse.

Related to this problem of a public presence, which is specially important for new plays, is the repertoire system. It is more difficult to catch a show that is in rep than in straight run, not necessarily for the devotee or loyal core audience but for the vital newcomer. The struggle to establish a new play and its characters — unnecessary for Shakespeare — is easier with consecutive performances. As it is, assuming that the planners have allowed enough previews for the cast to be confident they are presenting something worthwhile on the press night, it is then hard to sustain the momentum when they might not perform the show again for several days or even a couple of weeks, and may not have time for a word run because of other commitments. A cast has to grow into a new play during the run, and often reaches the right 'feel' only after several shows. If this process is interrupted too severely, such development is put in jeopardy.

Another unsettling side to this is the anomalies thrown up unexpectedly by the precarious nature of the RSC's 'success threshold'. The Company's ability to mount its operation depends on good accountancy and razor-sharp predictions of box-office takings. The margin of error is only a few per cent, beyond which adjustments have to be set in motion immediately. Such a situation effected all the productions in the autumn and winter of 1978, including *Shout Across the River,* which had been put forward when the film producer of *Scum* vetoed a stage performance. The Aldwych, with *Women Pirates* and *Cousin Vladimir,* had been doing badly, and then Mike Leigh cancelled his new show there. New work taking a hammering at the Aldwych hits The Warehouse box office, partly because tickets are sold for both theatres from the same spot; but when *As You Like It* came in to the Aldwych and picked up, so did The Warehouse, which gets the overspill when the main show is sold out. The rescheduling to meet this crisis kept Pete Atkin's *A and R* going for 41 performances, although it had been rushed into the repertoire, having been seen already in Edinburgh, when a commissioned play fell through. Compare this with the 19 performances of a new and commissioned play, *The Bundle.*

The situation gets worse when the logistics hit a play the other way round, and it gets fewer performances than expected or than is stated in the contract — a contractual minimum is usually 21 performances. This happened with *Men's Beano,* commissioned from Nigel Baldwin. The cast could not start rehearsals on time because of an overlap with *Once in a Lifetime,* which was due to open at the Aldwych first. Some previews of *Men's Beano* were therefore cancelled, and the opening night postponed — which is a bad start for any play, but particularly for a new one. When the director was able to start work, he was allocated different rehearsal spaces at different times, some distance from where the actors were rehearsing the Aldwych show. Then government cuts, the increase in Value Added Tax forcing up ticket prices, the Aldwych box office falling below par, and a tour to the US falling through, combined to produce the start of the Company's most serious crisis. The productions that could have dovetailed with *Men's Beano* did not survive the rescheduling, and it came off early after only twelve performances.

Generally speaking, the number of productions is worked out by matching up two sums, with variables on both sides. The number of productions needed to keep the revenue at its maximum, which is not necessarily the highest, is set against the number required to 'back' the shows in the larger theatre to produce the optimum returns. This time the system had been overloaded. The Warehouse had taken on too much, and in all the proceedings artistic values took and had to take second place to market forces.

The Warehouse 'pool' of writers

What clout do writers — the future life-blood of the theatre — have in all this? To the RSC, they must be as passing strangers, unless they have a long association with the Company, like Rudkin (and that has been painful), or have the weight of an Edward Bond. Yet similar 'heavyweights', like John Arden and Arnold Wesker, have run into deep difficulties with the RSC, which may make the commitment to writers look surprising. (Ironically, it was the row between Arden and Margaretta D'Arcy and the RSC over *The Island of the Mighty* that helped lead to the setting up of the Theatre Writers Group. As the Theatre Writers Union, it boycotted the National Theatre and, after two years of negotiations, agreed in 1979, alongside the Writers Guild, a minimum contract of £2,000 and certain rights over artistic decisions, royalties, and rehearsals, for any writer working with the RSC, the National, or the Royal Court.) One of the major points of conflict with the Ardens, the access of authors to rehearsals, has not, however, been a problem at The Warehouse, where the team has tried to build good and useful working relations with a growing number of playwrights. These can be divided at any one moment into those commissioned by the Company and those with whom The Warehouse shares a mutual interest — though by 1979 this contact had only stretched to seven women out of 67 writers.

As theatre is a practical art, the writers in The Warehouse 'pool' have been invited to see Warehouse shows and to find out about the space and the Company, in an attempt to make them feel involved with a practising theatre — a privilege shared, after all, with Shakespeare and Molière. None of the writers, though, has been seen as the 'property' of The Warehouse or been discovered there, though in the same period there were precious few 'discoveries' anywhere, at a time when the Royal Court and the National were not pursuing a consistent policy towards new writing, and theatres like the Half Moon were getting fixed in an experimental style dominated by the director rather than the playwright. The Warehouse has not wanted to abandon writers like Barker, Keeffe, or Baldwin just because they are not 'new'. Their *work* is new, and their canvas cannot always be accommodated by other theatres. Likewise, commitment to a writer must stretch beyond one play, which may or may not work as well as everyone had hoped, because playwriting, like all crafts, takes time to develop. For example, whatever the shortcomings of *The Innocent* may have been, working at The Warehouse gave Tom McGrath a confidence in his own voice and a social perspective that was missing from his earlier plays like *The Hardman*.

However, the pressure of the 'sausage factory' system is all too real, and can make it difficult to find the time to iron out important artistic problems with writers. Some of these problems should be foreseen before the actors start rehearsing, others do not always become clear until the play reaches the rehearsal floor — and then, despite the relative luxury of a long rehearsal period at The Warehouse, they do not always get solved. Writers take a big risk, and they can be damaged by having a play put on before it is ready. They also need a challenge to avoid falling into a mould, and that has sometimes been lacking. The value of the commissioning system at The Warehouse, however, is that work can be seen within three months of being written, which is important for freshness and topicality, and any rewriting can be done while the initial impetus can still be sustained.

Commissioning also brings much-needed, though insufficient, money to hard-pressed writers. The fee at The Warehouse in its first three seasons was on average £750 — peanuts for the time it takes to research and write a play. In any case, very few writers can afford to live off writing for the stage. However, commissioning has its problems: some writers do not like to write to deadlines, and even less to a subject. Others may agree, and then not come up with the goods, or may produce a script that is not up to standard. Commissioning is a gesture of trust in the writer. There are serious consequences if it is not honoured in full, as with *Men's Beano* — or, worse, if it is not honoured at all, as happened with *Carnival War a Go Hot* by Michael Hastings (eventually taken up by the Royal Court Theatre Upstairs), the only case in the first three years.

In late 1979, in the face of the worsening economic crisis and the new Theatre Writers Union contract, managerial pressure was exerted inside the RSC to stop commissioning and to buy only existing scripts.

This broke with the philosophy of The Warehouse and implied a consensus rather than a creative approach to new writing. It would jeopardize the RSC's relationship with a writer like Howard Barker, who had a third play performed at The Warehouse in 1980 and a new play for the Aldwych, or David Edgar, who came back from a year in the US in November 1979 and started work on adapting *Nicholas Nickleby* for the Aldwych's next season.

Most frustrating for The Warehouse, though, as for any theatre concerned with new writing, is knowing that the number of writers that can be coped with is but a drop in a vast and deep ocean. As Nunn has said: 'The heart of a nation's drama must be measured by the amount of new plays being written — the heart of a nation's theatre by the number being done'. British playwriting is still highly regarded throughout the world, and the Theatre Writers Union alone has more than 250 members. Add to the number of professionals the hundreds of enthusiasts who send in scripts, and it can be understood why the RSC receives on average twelve plays a week to read. The Warehouse programme for any one season only has one slot alongside the commissioned plays for scripts that come in out of the blue — though the proportions will change as the cost of commissioning goes up.

This situation led to The Warehouse holding a series of public play-readings, not as try-outs for a full production (though *Captain Swing* did get taken up by this route), but simply to give a few more writers the chance to see their work performed before an audience. Discussions, often led by a critic, followed the readings. Walter Donohue, who set up the readings as part of his responsibility to writers, is the first to say that much more needs to be done. He and Howard Davies have tried to make the system work at The Warehouse, and to open up the RSC through participation in the National Student Drama Festival, the Greater London Arts Association Playwriting Competition, and the Susan Blackburn Prize for women writers. But resources are overstretched, and the commissioning budget is not high enough to allow flexibility when things go wrong.

Pressure from production managers increased in 1979, and the relative isolation of The Warehouse within the Company became more of a problem as the crisis sharpened. Reorganization at the end of 1979 and the start of 1980, which involved one involuntary redundancy, was intended to give the Warehouse more clout, so as to enable it to play its part inside the RSC more fully, but the changes were made to meet managerial rather than artistic needs. Far-reaching action was still required to create a situation in which the moment that was right for the dramatist was also the moment that was right for the Company.

6. The work on Shakespeare

The new work at The Other Place and The Warehouse has to be seen in the context of the RSC as a whole, not just in terms of how human and material resources are used, but also in terms of content, style, and repertoire. Although almost any play can be staged in almost any space, some are obviously more suited to one kind of theatre than to another. Most farces, for example, require a single focus for the action — which has to be seen by the audience from the same direction, and is therefore less likely to be suited to a theatre-in-the-round than a proscenium. In the case of the RSC's 'other spaces', most of the new plays could have been staged as effectively in other acting areas and to larger audiences — which is not to detract from the RSC productions or from the particular experience of seeing them 'close-up'. However, what was unique to the small-theatre space as a space, and not just as an available outlet, was the new work on Shakespeare, as Buzz Goodbody had realized. The Other Place's distinctive Shakespeare style was created in the first three seasons by *Lear, Hamlet,* and *Macbeth,* which form a group, complementing and commenting on each other.

The focus for each, as the titles suggest, is a significant individual, but in the three productions none is a hero, none a victim — all are of noble birth and either rule, are born to rule, or become a ruler — and, although in some way alienated, none acts in isolation. All are shown to the audience through their actions, for which they are responsible, and which define their relationships to their society, to their peers and, most important, to their family. In each case, Shakespeare is seen to have created a real, believable, convincing world — including ghosts and witches. Together, the three brisk, business-like productions add up to a powerful, moral exploration of a terrorized, treacherous society that is cynical, brutish, and brutalizing — not far from the world of Barker, Brenton, or Bond. Yet a spark of hope always remains.

Lear as domestic tragedy

Lear, which was only the third Shakespeare Buzz Goodbody had directed, started life as an education programme, with selected speeches and scenes from the play alongside other material — an idea that owed a lot to John Barton's influence. By the time the production opened the only sign of such origins was a prologue, spoken by the actors playing Lear and Edgar, about poverty and beggars, and even this was dropped after fifteen performances. Produced for schools,

Lear was performed by a cast of nine, with one musician playing gong, trumpet, snare, and kettle drum. An all-purpose servant was added, while one sub-plot was cut (losing Albany, Cornwall, Oswald, and the French King), along with any lines that its characters had to say in other scenès. No cuts were made on grounds of comprehension, unlike most productions, including Brook's — indeed, the part of Lear was probably the fullest ever played by the RSC.

The programme, which paid tribute to Brook, admitted the losses in the text, but failed to spell out boldly enough the thinking behind the production. It was seen in London (at The Place) and in the US, and the same version has been performed in Australia, with Lear played by Warren Mitchell, who had been inspired by the RSC production. It has also been used in education work undertaken by RSC members. The acting area was empty, except for a few props, like a rug and banners which unfurled when Lear appeared. The gangways in the three-sided auditorium were utilized throughout, particularly in the fight between Edgar and Edmund. Scenes were set simply, using props and, as with the storm, music and lights, which at key moments in the production underscored the director's point. Thus, when Gloucester's first eye was plucked, half the lights were put out, and on the second there was a full blackout. The audience sniffed and smelled its way to Dover with him. Equally basic was the hunting of Edgar, the image of opposition: tracked with spotlights like an animal, his almost naked body was smeared all over with mud. Most crucially, the lights came up full for the Fool, who was played in a music-hall tradition, as a popular moral commentator, when he made his Albion speech about the state of the nation (a link with *Bingo*).

Lear was not seen as epic in terms of great public scenes of wide-open spaces peopled with a huge cast, but in its approach and scope. In fact, its focus was on two families, in which the personal as well as the age differences played a more important part than is usually recognized. Edgar's madness was very much a condition caused by his believing his father had rejected him, and a representation of the social consequences of that, which was what lay at the root of Edmund's climb to power — the driving force of the plot. In this land soldiered by sinister men in iron masks, who may have killed the Fool, Edmund was the one who played the game until the system beat him, taking on this role from the Bastard in *King John*.

Lear's family was seen in its closeness, with the daughters, who were no ugly sisters from a fairy tale ancient Britain, waiting on him hand and foot, loving him and hating him, and 'deceiving' him to survive, as only seemed sensible in the circumstances. Tony Church did not play Lear as a virtuoso acting part, but as a down-to-earth king, a patriarch who got his pleasure from hunting. He is out in the cold because of who he is — not a mighty monarch fallen from grace, but an old man on the point of death, facing himself and his life (a theme that tied in with *Babies Grow Old* in the same season). When he is 'sane', he represents the cruel world, arbitrary and aggressive, and only when he is 'mad' does he embody human values — an artistic device which Brecht was to use in *The Good Person of Szechwan* and *Puntila*.

In rehearsal, Buzz Goodbody was concerned to overcome the preconceptions that she thought schools audiences would bring to the production. *King Lear* had not been performed in Stratford since 1968, and she knew it had to be clear, exciting, and fresh. The pace had to be swift, which meant great attention to getting each scene to be true and forceful, and each one to follow the next as if no other could. The audience had to be carried along, step by step, but without their knowing it. She held improvisations, related to the play and not as an end in themselves, to capture what is was like in a family — the daughters being 'sired' by a crusty, selfish father, what to do with parents when they are old, and, particularly, how to cope with the sexual tensions, like incest.

Buzz Goodbody was worried that this side of *Lear* would have suffered in the classroom, especially in girls' schools. As in most Shakespeare, sexuality goes deep, but is often avoided in production — and more so in teaching — or is accommodated as coy, romantic, or a romp. She took solo sessions with the daughters and Tony Church, who had to shut his eyes and explore their bodies with his hands, describing what he felt as their father Lear: they went as far as forcing Goneril's legs apart when Lear curses her womb, to drive the point home. Other moments were highlighted to show sexual attraction as a motor in the play. Edmund (Charles Dance), who was also involved in body-contact exercises in which the actors made love without words, stroked the face of someone in the audience during his first speech, and Goneril (Sheila Allen) took off a stocking for him. Each rehearsal session would end with the whole team, including the technical staff and any visiting directors like Nunn, sitting in a circle discussing the work. Everyone's opinion was asked for and encouraged. People brought along their own research material — for example, on madness, for which a psychologist was also consulted.

A 'village-hall' Hamlet

The same rehearsal method was used in *Hamlet*. The aim was again to challenge every actor on every line, and to make what was happening before the audience as real as what happened on the rehearsal floor. This meant the director creating an atmosphere of hard, busy, and creative work, in which the actors could find the confidence to explore themselves, their beliefs, their strengths and weaknesses, and to follow the logic of their discovery as far as possible in terms of the play. At the first rehearsal, before the cast had met each other, Buzz Goodbody made them act *Hamlet* in five minutes, led by the Player King (Bob Peck). This turned out to be the basis for the dumb show in the production — an almost agitprop performance in white masks, played with a sexual rhythm to the beat of a drum.

It was also during rehearsal that the idea arose for a village hall set — a raised but shallow platform against white screens, ramps at the side, and a Kabuki-style bridge running through the audience to the rear. The screens served as the arras, and clicked back and forth like a camera shutter for the entrances and exits which overlapped like baton changers in a relay race. Chris Dyer's more or less monochrome design was as hard and clean as the action, which was staged in modern dress: as he puts it, 'an expensive show looking worn, not a cheap show looking dear'. (Costume finish in the small spaces has to be good because of the close-up relationship.) The design also allowed immediacy, involving the audience but not interfering with them as in *Lear*. Hamlet could always keep the audience in view, and sit on the edge of the stage, talking to them as his confidants. They became the court, or, in the vein of the pin-striped Claudius, shareholders at a company annual general meeting. As in *Lear,* the action took place all round, and when Laertes returned to Elsinore the doors of the theatre really shook.

The staging encouraged simple but brilliant effects, like the disappearance of the ghost. The audience is watching Hamlet speak to his father. They have to turn their heads to see him reply, because he is standing behind them. They turn their heads again to see Hamlet and after his reply turn back to the ghost, who has gone. Another product of collective rehearsal was the final scene, which, despite breaking into a savage brawl when the foil trick is discovered, had a clarity that came out of anarchic, improvised, Keystone Cops-type chases. Some of the cast also visited the London School of Economics to get the atmosphere of modern student life, but such exercises were never games. They helped provoke consequences for the production, as company 'feeling' was built (with difficulty) and developed through its own discoveries within a framework defined by the director. The exercises also helped the cast to see *Hamlet* through contemporary eyes, getting as far away from the fustian tradition as possible without destroying the play.

The influence on the production of T. S. Eliot was clear, as was that of Camus' *The Myth of Sisyphus* — which examines suicide, and concludes that life can be worth living despite its absurdity if it is lived in consciousness of that absurdity. Ben Kingsley's Hamlet, then, was distinguished by his consciousness and not just by his birth. Back from the best university, with his searing eyes and tightly-sprung gestures, he could see all that was sick in the menacing, corrupt, claustrophobic state. His Mancunian companion, Horatio, could not, yet Hamlet relied on him, although the prince could not believe that true friendship was possible in a society based on reason but which resolved its problems by violence. Trapped in a Kafka-like system, how was Hamlet to act under these circumstances, without becoming equally a brute?

He never took the easy course, like killing Claudius when he came across him alone and unsuspecting. The contradictions Hamlet felt, which for him defined the limits of theory and practice, were the social roots of his 'madness'. Like Lorenzaccio in Paul Thompson's adaptation of Alfred de Musset's play performed at The Other Place in 1977, Hamlet found that there were no individual answers, however remarkable a person one might be. Fortinbras, dressed for war, shattered the fragile alliance between the military and the politicians, and at the end the sound of marching feet was heard as he swept on — Hamlet and his class lying dead on the stage.

Claudius (George Baker) was played as a Nixon figure, whose hunting of Hamlet became the mechanism of the narrative. Yet Claudius realized that he also was trapped in the system he had created, which could only lead to a bloody end. He wanted to stop it but could not, and death offered the only release. Polonius (André van Gyseghem) was modelled on Macmillan — with his own sense of humour, and by no means a fool. For example, he was the only one to recognize the crucial role of neglected love in Hamlet's condition. His perception, however, did not come from his being a bright senior civil servant and the king's closest adviser, but out of his own close family ties. *Hamlet*, like *Lear,* is a story about two families. Again, a lot of work went into the domestic aspect, linking it to the political and the social.

The neglected love was made real, and Hamlet, for once, had a convincing relationship both with his mother Gertrude and with Claudius, into whose arms she returned immediately after the bedroom scene. The spur in Hamlet's side was his attachment to his father, whose appearance as a ghost was made credible as an image in his son's mind. There were no funny sound or lighting effects. He was flesh and blood as he stood behind Hamlet, clasping his hands over his son's head as he sat cross-legged on the floor. In contrast to the divided Hamlet family, Polonius, Laertes, and Ophelia made a loving, caring family group, who were genuinely affectionate. This made sense of the madness of Ophelia — wearing her dead father's dressing gown and her face disfigured with lipstick — and of Laertes' grief, which Claudius exploits to set the two sons against each other, both obsessed by their father's murder but reluctant to take revenge.

Yet Polonius still had one set of rules for his daughter and another for his son, and extended his concerns of state to have his son spied upon. Betrayal was a key theme in the production, made all the more intense because it sprang not just from friends but from family. Like the viciousness towards women, it was not carried out by baroque monsters but by well-dressed, well-mannered, smooth-tongued gentlemen in an apparently civilized society — snatches of Brahms were played offstage. Much was made of this during rehearsal in trust exercises, but it was a risky approach because it probed the vulnerable and touched on the painful as, for example, when Ben Kingsley had to think back to his childhood and incidents with his mother. And there was disagreement among the cast over some of the work — particularly one of the last exercises, when Ophelia was carried up the river bank in Stratford in a funeral procession, and a grave was dug for her.

It was in this production more than in any other that Buzz Goodbody found the excitement of making dangerous connections. This certainly gave the show a burning quality, and produced a rare tension more akin to a gripping whodunnit than a classic. The actors gave not just good but unexpected performances, yet the price of that experiment was very high. Buzz Goodbody worked closely on Shakespeare's language and on understanding the text, which was largely uncut. She tried to make sense of the play in Elizabethan terms and at the same time translate it into her own. Thus, her belief in control of the body, including the voice — her sessions began with physical exercises led by different people in turn — helped Ben Kingsley develop his verbal dexterity (which prepared him for parts like Mosca at the National). The cast learnt that fast speech could propel ideas as well as, if not better than, laborious punctuation, swilling the words in the mouth, or 'navel contemplation'. They took their cue from Hamlet's advice to the players, and avoided the 'poetic' in order to speak as easily as Shakespeare wrote, without losing the quality of the text. This led to great vocal variation, quick changes of tone, and new interpretations — like the Player King delivering his dramatic speech in a low key, or the gravediggers' scene being played with natural humour and song, and not as a pantomime interlude with country bumpkins.

It was a self-mocking production, full of surprising and often-neglected humour. It was fervid and fluent, and had you on the edge of your seat from the moment it started with twelve bells and a darkness only broken by the pencil beam of a soldier's torch. Here was a most exciting and challenging new look at an old play, and a daring use of the intimate relationship between audience and performance, just as the rehearsal period had been between actor and director. Above all, it was a culmination and vindication of all of Goodbody's work, in the face of both what she felt Stratford had become and what many on the 'fringe' said it could never be.

Macbeth as a journey of the imagination

Buzz Goodbody did not live to see the great critical acclaim that greeted the production, which Nunn took over. He called it 'the most convincing *Hamlet* that I have ever seen', and it made a great impression on him, particularly when he came to work on *Macbeth* at The Other Place. In 1974, he had directed a 'good versus evil' production at the RST, set in a church. During rehearsal, he and designer John Napier had conceived a rostrum as the focus of action, but the proportions that were necessary for it to work on the stage meant that anyone not on the platform became virtually an outcast. The achievements of the rehearsal period in the Conference Hall, when Nunn had decided that the audience must experience the play at the same close quarters, were lost when the actors had to perform on the set of the large stage. In a production intended to be devoid of illusion, actors were forced to compensate for the loss of clarity and atmosphere by falling back on tricks of the trade, and the tendency of the proscenium arrangement to draw attention to form rather than content was increased.

Nunn reworked the production for the Aldwych transfer the following year. He replaced the rostrum by a black circle and kept the heavy furniture and props which played an important part in the ritual, representing both the real and imagined world of Macbeth. But Nunn knew that was not the end of it, and when Ian McKellen said he wanted to act at The Other Place in the 1976 season Nunn offered him Macbeth. To partner the surging, unpredictable style of McKellen, Nunn chose a brilliant naturalistic actress, Judi Dench. Her experience with Shakespeare's comic roles proved invaluable in helping create as credible a world as possible, where even the witches would not be out of place — and, because of that, would be even more threatening.

Nunn's only previous chamber work had been on *Dr. Faustus,* when he took it over in Dublin. But he had been fired by *Hamlet,* and, with most of the cast, felt he was now exploring new territory. Again, all the elements of the drama were important and played their part — jangling music, metal clashing in the fight, the scraping of spurs and boots, the thud of the dagger in the wooden floor, and sparing use of blood on Lady MacDuff's throat as it was slit just before a blackout. Macbeth was in black, Duncan in white, the others in dark greens and browns, denoting rank and character but without pre-empting the actor. The time was vague — about turn-of-the-century, with military men in breeches and knee-length boots. The actors sat inches away from the audience on upturned beer crates spaced out around a black circle painted in the centre of the bare, unpolished floorboards. Props were in full view at the side. The actors were all equal, and nothing happened until the audience had settled, and thereby signalled that they were ready to set off on the journey, as equals also. It was a journey of the imagination, exploring, appropriately, the power of Macbeth's mind to do what he fancied, and the discovery of its limitations, which were bound up with the individual's relationship to self, and of self to society.

As in *Lear* and *Hamlet,* the family was central to this exploration of a moral system and the consequences of breaking its codes. The play abounds with references to family and reproduction, and they form the narrative spine of the action — which in this production was played without break to heighten and make complete the experience and involvement of the audience. Despite being Shakespeare's shortest 'tragedy', Nunn still cut it, but this helped achieve the overall rhythm of the piece, which (characteristically of The Other Place) was made up of well-defined, dovetailed scenes that swiftly followed the one from the other in the best storytelling tradition.

Hard-faced Lady Macbeth, her hair scarfed tightly out of sight, had the warm-blooded precision of a killer tiger. The sensual relationship between 'Mr. and Mrs. Macbeth' played an important part in the murder of Duncan, as the courageous commander in the field had to prove himself as much 'a man' in the home. She tried hard to protect the image of their marriage when Macbeth saw Banquo's ghost at the feast, and her 'madness' was linked to the final break-up of that marriage, just as Macbeth's end was tied to the violation of the Macduff family and the survival of Banquo's seed. Macbeth the betrayer, stripped of self-respect and yet still a human being in whom the audience could recognize something of themselves, was surrounded at the end by an almost anonymous, swaying chorus — a circle of hell of his own creation. The carnage left the exhausted victors aghast, and, as with Fortinbras, suggested little confidence in the new rulers bringing the golden times of which they talked.

The production of *Macbeth* had an extremely strong cast that provided, with the *Destiny* company, the backbone of the opening season at The Warehouse. It was important, not just because of its tremendous success (playing also at the Gulbenkian Studio Theatre in Newcastle, the RST, The Warehouse, The Young Vic, and on commercial television), but also because the survival of the company spirit, and of the show itself in the different venues, was another vindication of the small-space experience. The Thames TV programme, which was not simply a recording but especially recreated for the small screen, could not capture the power and excitement felt in the theatre, and the run at the RST (during which incidentally the cast refused to follow normal dressing room allocation, which would have destroyed the rough democracy backstage at The Other Place) could not reach the intensity, immediacy, and contact of the small auditorium.

A tradition of 'chamber' classics

Hamlet and *Macbeth* both played in London at the same time as National Theatre productions that, ironically, were directed by the original architect of the RSC, Peter Hall. Sadly, the Hall productions showed that he had spent his energies and had not been able to develop with the times, whereas his old organization had. It was not surprising, therefore, to find that Hall had announced a desire to return to small-scale work to find himself again. The Other Place had pointed the way. In its first three years, the RSC had presented there a *Lear* which was the most challenging production of the play since Brook's over ten years before; a *Hamlet* which was to the 1970s what the Hall-Warner production was to the 1960s, and in many ways offered much more; and a *Macbeth* which, having penetrated the media more than the other two, achieved legendary status in its own lifespan.

These productions had brought Shakespeare full circle since his own day back to simple, straightforward playing that gave full rein to the imagination of both actors and audience. This approach implied a social as well as an artistic preference, as did the way an Irving, Kean, or Macready chose to stage Shakespeare, or nearer our time, a Wolfit. Lighting, scenery, props, costume, acting, all advanced the tragic or heroic individual and 'star' as the carrier of the play's meaning, and implied that only 'heroic' or at least important individuals made history. William Poel's garden productions, modern attempts to recreate the Elizabethan theatre, or the BBC television series of all Shakespeare's plays, reflected attitudes no less different in purpose from those that formed The Other Place 'tradition'.

At The Other Place, as at The Warehouse, social philosophy was in harmony with the artistic values of the most effective productions, expressed, for example, in the direct contact between performance and audience, or in the bare circle set that reappeared in *Pericles*. John Barton's lucid and rigorous re-examination of *The Merchant of*

69

Venice restated this forcefully. Patrick Stewart's hard-headed Shylock, rolling his own cigarettes, was a businessman who had to learn the art of survival in an aggressive and morally decadent society. Proud, rational, human, he was forced to bow to the reality of the Christian mercantile system, which is shown up by the contrast with isolated Belmont where the values of that system flourish, notably those of the property-based law, which regulates relationships between people. The unpleasant result shows the discrepancies and discriminations that affect those who do not have Portia's privileges.

The value of The Other Place in offering a new look at classical work raised the possibility of yet another theatre in Stratford to cope with many activities, including local events, but mainly devoted to the largely unexplored canon of non-Shakespearian Elizabethan and Jacobean plays. The Other Place can hardly touch on this collection because of its repertoire, which is limited by its restricted licence. But it would cost too much to bring The Other Place into line with the requirements of a full licence, particularly in terms of fire and storage, and planning permission is unlikely. The new theatre, scheduled to be run by Jean Moore, will seat 380, and is to be built out of the so-called Conference Hall, the shell of the original Memorial Theatre auditorium that was opened on Shakespeare's birthday in 1879 and burnt out in 1926.

This hall was where Nunn had experienced the excitement of *Macbeth* before its unsatisfactory transfer to the large stage, and the idea of a third auditorium had begun to take shape. His work on Ben Jonson's *The Alchemist* convinced him further. For example, it showed that realism can also work for comedy. Not an obvious choice for The Other Place, the play offered little room for interpretation, since it depends a lot on all the audience seeing certain things, like someone coming through a door, simultaneously and from a shared viewpoint. This was proven when the production transferred so successfully to the Aldwych — it had been difficult to redesign the set for The Warehouse, and a slot had fallen vacant in the larger theatre. The Other Place had allowed Nunn to play *The Alchemist* 'for real', and to cut through the usual preoccupation with humours and Jonsonian style that arises from an elaborate text. The thought of experimenting on other plays of the period was both exciting and a challenge for the future.

7. Writers of the twentieth century

Apart from plays by Shakespeare and his contemporaries, all the work staged at The Other Place has been from the present century, and here a distinctive contribution has been the re-examination of plays by established, dead playwrights, notably Brecht — with *Man is Man, Schweyk in the Second World War,* and *Baal* — but also Chekhov and O'Neill. Revivals of plays by living writers which might not otherwise be seen outside student productions — for example, Bond's *Bingo,* Wood's *Dingo,* and Brenton's *The Churchill Play* — have also formed a part of the programme. A unique service, however, was to help David Rudkin come in from the cold and find his voice in the theatre again.

New looks at Brecht, Bond, and Brenton

As with the Elizabethan and Jacobean work, the main advantage of the small-space modern 'classics' was clarity, especially in the productions of Brecht, whose plays are dogged by different interpretations because of his complex and contradictory texts. The three episodic, anti-naturalistic pieces suited the laboratory nature of the small theatres, and ranged from the cool approach of Howard Davies in the first two productions to David Jones's more flamboyant *Baal.* Each of the productions stressed the concern of all three plays to look at the individual in a new light and relationship to society: Baal, the anti-romantic poet and wanderer, whose life of sensual pleasures expresses openly what the ruling class prefers to keep hidden and separate; Galy Gay in *Man is Man,* the docker who is made by other men into a perfect fighting machine in an imperialist world that exists by re-assembling human beings as if they were cars; and Schweyk, the reverse of the eternal little man, who 'knows the score' and survives — which is both why groups like the nazis can come to power and why they will be defeated and outlived.

Here was Brecht showing the opposite of the Shakespearian individual, and yet the RSC productions of both were of a piece — an indication of Brecht's influence, his conscious link between the way you see the world and the way you present what you see. This can be traced in shows such as Pam Gems's *Piaf,* also directed by Davies, in which a compact, fluid, and funny production, mixing song and speech with props and costume changes in full view, placed the individual's struggles in their social context, avoiding sentimental biography without losing the personal angle through which the audience could enter the world of social analysis.

Davies and the designer Chris Dyer developed a hard, clipped style in the small spaces which worked most effectively in the first productions of Edward Bond, a playwright who comes very close to Brecht's concerns. With *The Bundle*, specially written for The Warehouse, the small space helped Bond's foreign world become 'real' in its own terms, and thus a more accurate tool for looking at our own society. The play had moved away from the individual to pose starkly the issue of morality and power — earlier explored in *Bingo* in a production that caught the play's different mood, while showing a continuity which was underlined by the same actor, Patrick Stewart, playing both Basho and Shakespeare, the artists at the centre of the respective plays, whose 'enlightenment' is ironically brought into question.

Davies focused *Bingo* more closely than the original production, and had Shakespeare more down-to-earth. With obvious irony for the RSC, Davies showed the dilemma of the great dramatist to be much more cruel and relevant — he cannot reconcile the justice he promotes in his plays with the injustice he is involved in as an accomplice of land enclosures. His way out is death. Yet our culture, which still promotes those same notions of justice, is built out of that same injustice of the landgrabbers — a point made more clearly in *The Bundle*. Here, the 'enlightenment' of the peasants comes from working with the available tools, weapons, and knowledge to bring social relations into line with their own moral values.

Barry Kyle's two revivals, of *The Churchill Play* and *Dingo*, both designed by Kit Surrey, also revealed a continuity. Both were played vigorously, the first with great attention to detail and realism, the second rooted in reality but flying high into a brash, vaudeville cruelty. The different styles were both satirical — Charles Wood's linguistic, comic fireworks gaining in force through the concentration of the small space that had been turned into a barbed-wire stage, whereas Brenton's carefully structured language, which showed the brutalizing effect of contemporary life, no longer sounded artificial, as it had when first played in 1974, but had become alarmingly 'natural'. Kyle exploited well the central image of the plays, which turns on its head the idea of prisoners putting on a play in order to escape. This has become almost a 'folk myth', symbolizing the good old values that made Britain great.

In *Dingo*, the myth, and the official history that accompanied it, were undermined, most sharply by the manic performance of Ian McDiarmid as the Comic. In *The Churchill Play*, the myths were exploded because it is 'our chaps' who are now running the concentration camp, which, after all, the British invented. The coffin draped with the Union Jack took on an oppressive, dominating presence in the small, bare space, and the romantic gesture at the end, when the civilian internees fight back against the totalitarian system, was certainly overpowering, however inadequate it may otherwise seem as a conclusion.

A creative catalyst for David Rudkin

Although the distinctive quality of the new plays presented at the two theatres lies in their content, there is one writer whose creative development has been shaped by his experience of working in the small space, and by his relationship to the director of that space, Ron Daniels. It took a forthright Buzz Goodbody to persuade David Rudkin to let *Afore Night Come* be staged again by the RSC, but when it was, like *The Churchill Play*, it seemed more 'real' and up-to-date than when it had first been produced. Its macabre side, along with worlds ruled by strict rituals and codes built into their language, surfaced again in the mammoth *The Sons of Light,* Rudkin's second stage play written a couple of years after *Afore Night Come* (he had tried his hand at television in between).

Both Peter Hall and Clifford Williams, who had directed the first *Afore Night Come*, looked at *The Sons of Light*, but there were disagreements which led to an eight-year gap in the relationship between Rudkin and the RSC. This was bridged by the Casement play at The Place in 1973, and more importantly by Buzz Goodbody's approach to Rudkin to direct *Afore Night Come* at The Other Place. He declined, but agreed to let the play be produced, though he had worries about being known as a one-play writer. However, Daniels's production acted as a catalyst for Rudkin, who had been on the verge of giving up writing for the stage, and it helped forge the close working relationship with Daniels that continued with *The Sons of Light* and *Hippolytus.*

Rudkin had put away *Sons* several times, and had rewritten it as many. After Keith Hack had directed a rather hallucenogenic production of it in Newcastle, Rudkin and Daniels came up with a version (which the author says will be his last), working on it together first in a dressing room at The Other Place and then in Rudkin's van in the car park outside. As in *Afore Night Come,* sacrifice is a strong element in the psychoanalytical labyrinth of the play, the central images of which are split into two — the island, guarded by a fortress, with its pit below, and the child Manatond, like Edgar in *Lear,* whose struggle for self, at the core of which is her sexuality, is mirrored in the moral drive to make sense of the world by joining up its parts and making of them one whole.

73

The play explores the workings of power, domination, and choice. The apparent lawlessness of the island community is deceptive to the stranger — but the policemen are inside their heads. This same 'enemy within' is the key to *Hippolytus*, another classic reclaimed for a modern audience through the severity of interrogation demanded by the small spaces. Rudkin has shifted the responsibility away from the gods to the humans, and the emphasis away from Phaedra to the repressed sexuality of Theseus' son. As with the Shakespeare productions at The Other Place, the result was to provide, in Rudkin's words, 'an English experience, not a Greek one'. A classical scholar, Rudkin had translated Greek plays before, and felt that the RSC should tackle them — which Barton had long wanted to do before his chance came with *The Greeks* in 1980.

Rudkin worked with The Other Place in mind — a space where the actors had to be recognizable, concrete, and specific. He went through the text, line by line with Daniels — this time they had been elevated to Nunn's office — marking any passages they could not agree upon, and coming back the next day with those parts rewritten. During rehearsal, Rudkin sat with the original Euripides while the actors used his text, so that he could show how honest to the original his 'realization' was — but on his own terms, the terms of the late 1970s. *Hippolytus* asked much the same questions as *Sons:* how to place human beings in their proper relation to each other and to the universe? *Sons* had pushed the use of the small spaces further than any other production; Daniels and the actors had carved a clear narrative path through a bizarre and fantastic world created through lights, sounds, and Ralph Koltai's gravel and plastic design. *Hippolytus* was the reverse — a simple unobstructed debate with the audience, played in white costumes behind low rails against a beaten tin background.

Social naturalism and political realism

The style which was evolved to present Rudkin's philosophy did give the production a precious, holy feeling, which was quite the opposite of the abrasive quality associated with The Warehouse — not just in the rhetorical work of Barker and Brenton, but in that large group of plays that have most exploited naturalistic elements. Rudkin was saying that the universe could never be encompassed by man's descriptions of it, but the writers presented at The Warehouse concentrated on a rather different universe — an immediate, and increasingly run-down and hostile environment. A link with Rudkin remained, in that political systems and institutions were seen as surviving by taking away from people the responsibility for their lives — and this accounts for much of the desperation portrayed in plays

like *The Innocent, Savage Amusement, Men's Beano, Look Out* . . .
Here Comes Trouble, and *Shout Across the River.* This is also seen as
working at the personal level: individuals survive by taking away from
other individuals the responsibility for their lives.

But few of the writers have tackled this head on in its most basic
contemporary aspect, the ways in which men act to oppress women.
Of the writers chosen for the two theatres, only Pam Gems and
Howard Brenton have put the issue at the heart of plays, although
women were central characters in *Shout* by Poliakoff and *Look Out*
by O'Malley. Unfortunately, Gems's *Queen Christina* was a troubled
production, and it was the only show, apart from *The Shepherd's Play*
(which toured locally at Christmas in 1978), that was not brought to
London, though it was seen in Newcastle. And Brenton's *Sore
Throats* was a male fantasy of women's sexual liberation.

Gems has fewer illusions about the possibilities of liberation, given
the pressures of the society Brenton himself so caustically attacks, and
in *Queen Christina* and in *Piaf* she looks at the problems of fighting
back against the roles women are expected to play. Christina, who
lived at the time Shakespeare was writing *As You Like It* (the play
which was 'twinned' with Gems's in Stratford), was brought up to be
a man so that she could fulfil her royal duties. But she wanted to live
and rule as a woman. Did she have to follow men's habits because it
was a man's world? The issue becomes sharper because she cannot fall
back on traditional ways out, like using her 'looks'. Unlike the Garbo
cinema image, Christina was slightly hunched and did not conform to
any standards of conventional beauty. How could she be herself? That
same question dominates *Piaf,* which shows, with unsentimental
triumph, a woman at the other end of the social scale who, despite at
one time being the highest-paid singer in the world, stayed true to her
roots.

The choice of new plays reflected an approach to theatre that
matched the small-space philosophy. Although they could all have been
played in larger auditoria, as some were (including *Piaf* in the West
End), few would have stayed the course in box-office terms. Some did
benefit particularly from the conditions of the RSC and its other spaces,
like Edgar's *The Jail Diary of Albie Sachs,* which he was asked to adapt
for The Warehouse after the success of *Destiny.* Apart from fitting in
with the other work on South Africa (a play about the Steve Biko
inquest, and a late-night show about expatriates living in England), *Jail
Diary* used the relationship between audience and actor in a very skilful
way. Davies's spare production and Dyer's open design removed any
barriers between the imprisoned lawyer and the audience, who were
inside the jail with Sachs, sharing his solitary confinement and asking
themselves the same questions about commitment. The production

allowed full rein to the central concern of the play and its motor force — the character of Sachs himself facing dilemmas and having to choose. The struggle since the Sharpeville Massacre and the growing repression against white as well as black meant that passive resistance was no longer effective. How would he, the audience, and the author cope with the new, harsh realities? The space emphasized this side of the play and permitted no hiding place.

With Peter Whelan's *Captain Swing* the space was right again, as the audience became villagers caught up in the swirl of radical ideas in the 1830s. The threshing floor of the Sussex village was the bare floor of the theatre, and the action took place all around, with plenty of flail, drum, and bugle sounds. It was an appropriate play for Stratford because the agricultural workers' union was founded nearby, and along with *The Bundle* this was the only play to centre on working people using their collective strength to try and win a better life. Bill Alexander's lively production did not overplay the contemporary parallels — which ranged from new technology battles and the media campaign against the unions to laws planned to take away some of the union rights which the Sussex labourers helped to establish. But it did contain stunning images of the equally topical problem of reformism, captured in dream-like tableaux and the ambiguity of the Swing figure, whose name was used to sign letters which fanned ruling-class fears about anarchy, in contrast to the labourers' orderliness and attachment to commonly-agreed procedures. One sequence, in particular, showed the power of ideas and the need to break with old ones, as a wooden Christ was sawn off its cross on an upper acting level, and taken down onto the ground to become the symbol of a new order, inspired by the French Revolution. The play ends with the words: 'What is this law the people keep . . . if they kill Swing . . . and those who govern break us?'

But mostly the nature of the spaces did not offer anything distinctive to what a play was saying — except, and most important, the chance to say it at all. David Edgar's *Destiny,* for example, which Daniels considers to be the prototype new play for The Other Place, started life quite specifically aimed at large stages with full-blown effects (it was no wonder, then, that you could bump into a meeting of fascists in the toilets at The Other Place).

Edgar, who had been a journalist, had spent a couple of years interviewing and researching the play, which charted how the ideas of the defeated nazis were re-asserted in British politics in the 30 years after the Second World War. In 1973, his first draft for David Hare, literary adviser to Richard Eyre at the Nottingham Playhouse, would have taken over five and a half hours to perform, a familiar 'get-it-all-in' problem with many left-wing playwrights. The prolific Edgar, who had seen the financial disaster of Portable Theatre touring a large-scale show, was keen, nevertheless, to have his work played on big stages in front of large audiences. As he says, 'battlefields are bigger than bedrooms', and he and his contemporaries, like Brenton and Barker, had been well served already by the 'fringe', but wanted to go beyond what it could offer.

Birmingham Rep said it was interested in a manageable version of *Destiny,* which is set in a fictional town to the west of Birmingham, but changed its mind when times were hard, preferring a smaller-cast play about an adolescent boy putting out the eyes of horses. Nottingham's plans fell through in 1975, Sheffield would not read the play, the National sent a personal 'no' from Peter Hall, and the RSC turned it down. Ironically, Edgar then turned down the RSC, when Daniels had persuaded Nunn to read the play, and to say 'yes'. Edgar did not want another small-theatre production, but changed his mind when he knew a second London auditorium was to be opened by the RSC.

However, when *Destiny* transferred, it went into the Aldwych, and the set of the so-called small space was too big to fit. There was little cash for the transfer, and the designer, Di Seymour, who had to cope with a permanent set for the Shakespeare plays, decided to make the *Destiny* design simpler, although the Birmingham text had included instructions for massive effects. Her point was proved when *Destiny* was broadcast to millions on BBC television, and concentration on the argument was made difficult by fussy sets. There were times, however, when the argument itself could only just be sustained by the agitprop structure of the play, which still bore the marks of Edgar's involvement with issue-plays and groups like General Will.

The RSC production gave a great boost to the anti-fascist and anti-racist movement, in which Edgar was active. Supporters of extreme right-wing groups interrupted the play at the Aldwych, though it was never attacked as has been Red Ladder in Leeds, or Recreation Ground when it was visiting Bradford, or the Albany Theatre which was 'mysteriously' burnt down. *Destiny* won Edgar the Arts Council's John Whiting Award for the best new play with contemporary relevance, and was certainly the most immediately political of any of the plays presented by the RSC in the 1970s. But it has been criticized on the left for its too 'passive' analysis — which Edgar describes as him being 'irresponsibly responsible', though in the television version he wrote in a strong speech by a trade unionist to clear up any doubts.

The nature of the new writing

That sort of political confusion was characteristic of many of the plays that were presented at the RSC's other spaces, particularly at

The Warehouse, and which could have been presented at various other similar venues, such as the Royal Court Theatre Upstairs, the Bush, or the Sheffield Crucible's studio. The majority of Warehouse plays were rooted in the urban underbelly of a decaying welfare state, and relied heavily on naturalism or naturalistic techniques, so that even a sympathetic critic like Michael Billington could caricature a typical Warehouse play as a species of latter-day 'kitchen sink' drama.

But the choice did represent a conscious approach, based on developing a relationship with writers rather than staging new work as such. This meant not only being concerned with the finished product but with the whole of the process of creating and putting on a play. It also meant excluding a range of drama, in terms both of topics and method: experimental performance and design, new ways of putting shows together, and non-verbal theatre, for example, found no place at The Warehouse. And the building proved less than suitable for certain comedies like *Look Out . . . Here Comes Trouble*, which would have happily found a place in a proscenium theatre.

Nor did the permanent seating permit different shapes for the acting area, such as was possible at the Royal Court Theatre Upstairs or the Cottesloe, where a 'house style' was developed through folksy 'promenade' productions, which certainly presented a view of the nation and its history quite at odds with that of The Warehouse. Here, there were no visions of Britain as one nation, with everyone in the same boat, whatever the differences. The world as seen at The Warehouse was becoming a colder place, torn apart by political, social, sexual, and mental strife as people came to terms with having little control over their lives, despite 30 or so post war years of apparent peace and prosperity.

A quotation from Gramsci aptly reflects the approach: 'The crisis persists precisely in the fact that the old is dying and the new cannot be born; in this interregnum a great variety of morbid symptoms appears'. The words of the poet Matthew Arnold, 'Wandering between two worlds, one dead/The other powerless to be born', were quoted by Howard Barker at the beginning of the text of *That Good Between Us,* which opened The Warehouse. His *The Hang of the Gaol* showed how the energy of a writer could be released through the discipline of a small-space production that made his challenge a burning one, even if it lacked direction. The closeness of the action focused the plays very sharply as moral attacks on the ideological power of the ruling class, which, as in *Swing,* backs up its cultural 'weaponry' with force. The zealous ex-Communist civil servant, unearthing the culprit who burnt down a famous gaol, knows that his individual crusade is doomed, and colludes with the authorities to get his knighthood instead.

Compromise keeps the hated system going, but failure to do anything leads to worse — as in *That Good*, in which a spy-mad special branch detective pushes a Labour government into introducing imprisonment without trial and even more authoritarian measures. But despite a strong journalistic element encouraged by the small spaces, none of the plays identified any forces capable of bringing about the long and short term changes that the writers would have liked to see in society, and, apart from *Destiny*, none confronted immediate political issues such as Northern Ireland, or the government's destruction of Britain's basic industries. Though the choices were getting starker, none of the writers, except for Bond, conceived of their plays in terms of solutions.

'Social awareness' had swept the theatrical board in the 1970s, trailing even light comedy in its wake, but the conservative mood at the end of the decade was more favourable to sophisticated 'boulevard' writers such as Tom Stoppard than to the Barkers, Brentons, or Edgars. Their names did not join Stoppard's in the neon lights of Shaftesbury Avenue, unlike their radical predecessors — Arnold Wesker, for example — who did win new and large audiences in Britain and abroad. A political writer was no longer an oddity, and the big names of the late 1950s and 1960s had either gone into 'exile' or not kept pace with the social conflicts that the RSC's other spaces gave voice to. However inadequate, it was important that this voice was heard, especially as it was getting increasingly difficult for it to be heard elsewhere. But such a situation posed new problems for the writers and those seeking a role for the other spaces in the 1980s, particularly as the left was weak and there was little public acceptance of a working-class, let alone of a revolutionary, cultural tradition to which they might aspire.

Conclusion

Despite ups and downs, the RSC won widespread critical acclaim in the 1970s which would not have been possible without the contribution and influence of its other spaces. They allowed many of the Company's ideas to be practised more consistently and effectively than in the larger theatres, whether in the exploration of the rehearsal period, the building of company feeling, the design, the direction, or the performance. At the smaller theatres, an identity and style was created to match the spaces and the audiences. It is doubtful whether Buzz Goodbody's *King John* would have been so savagely attacked if it had been performed at The Other Place, because of the different critical values and expectations there. Appropriately enough, the distinctive quality can be summed up from *Hamlet:* 'Let your own discretion be your tutor: suit the action to the word, the word to the action; with this special observance, that you o'erstep not the modesty of nature; for anything so overdone is from the purpose of playing, whose end, both at the first and now, was and is, to hold, as 'twere, the mirror up to nature; to show virtue her own feature, scorn her own image, and the very age and body of the time his form and pressure'.

The best productions at the other spaces were not metaphorical or metaphysical. Their truth was specific and arose out of a particular philosophy and the existence of an educated, critical audience that gave substance to that philosophy. Starting from scratch, the actor and audience constructed together the world of the play. Generalized gestures or emotion were out of place in that urgent search for meaning in an alienated, fragmented, class society. It was neither just the individual nor just the environment that was crucial, but the interaction of the two.

This social dimension was linked artistically to the advance of realism, as against the reproduction of surface reality, which can also be seen in the cinema and other arts — even in opera, particularly under the influence of theatre directors such as Peter Hall and William Gaskill. This dimension also requires an appropriate method of communication — acting, directing, design — conceived in terms of the closeness and scrutiny of the audience. The role of the audience and the relationship in the productions between language, imagination, and social values implied an act of faith in the capacity of human beings to understand, and therefore to act upon themselves and their situation (within the limits of their time and place). It also implied an act of faith in the social value of truth and knowledge, in the sharing of both, and, in that process, of taking control. Therefore, it was also an act of faith in democracy. At its best, and with all its limitations, it was theatre in and for an age of reason, science, and technology, in a century that saw both the birth of the first socialist societies and the creation of the means of total destruction.

The Newcastle seasons and small-scale tours

The opening of The Warehouse completed the RSC's renewal in the 1970s which started with The Other Place. Complementing these two 'fixed' features of the process were the trips to Newcastle upon Tyne and the small-scale tours. Newcastle provided a base in the north-east to add to the RSC's 'homes' in the Midlands and the south-east, and in 1980, for the first time, the Newcastle visit included more shows from the smaller Stratford space than from its 'main house'. Most important for the Company, however, were the mobile 'other spaces' — the small-scale tours which continued the search for new audiences (it's worth noting that 'small-scale' relates to the size of most of the venues, not to the extent of the territory covered). Theatregoround had died, and the RSC knew that it wanted something different to replace it. Television productions — *Antony and Cleopatra, Hedda Gabler, Destiny, Macbeth,* and *The Comedy of Errors* — though seen by millions, were one-offs, sometimes independently produced, and slotted into an evening's viewing alongside the channel's other programmes. *Henry V* had toured large cities in 1976, staying a week and moving on in traditional fashion. The Newcastle five-week season, which covered the spread of the RSC's work, replaced that form of touring, but still left many parts of Britain without an accessible visit by either of the national companies that are supported by everyone's taxes. It was, in the event, The Other Place which gave rise to the first small-scale tour from July to October 1978.

Regional arts associations, especially South-West Arts, had often asked for visits by the RSC, particularly since a misunderstanding involving the Arts Council in 1975 had led the administrators of some venues to believe that Buzz Goodbody's production of *Hamlet* at The Other Place was going to tour just when, to rub salt in the wound, it opened in London. One of the great successes of the 1978 tour was the time spent in the south west, in Cornwall — four shows playing over capacity in a gymnasium, and a morning workshop for 400 school children. The tour was organized by Jean Moore, 'on leave' from The Other Place; a third of the company, led by Ian McKellen, had worked on *Macbeth* at The Other Place; and Nunn went on from being artistic director at The Other Place to direct one of the tour productions, *The Three Sisters,* which played at The Other Place in 1979.

The shows were planned and produced in the style of The Other Place, opening up the company to reach new audiences through a re-examination of classics in 'close-up', using mobile, minimal scenery and props on a portable platform designed by John Napier with a cloth backdrop. The Chekhov, *Twelfth Night* directed by Jon Amiel, and an 'anthology-entertainment' about being English, *And is There Honey Still for Tea?*, devised by one of the tour actors, Roger Rees, were performed in 26 towns in England and Scotland. Only five of the venues, however, seated less than 350 people, and too many were part of the arts centre circuit, mainly because of inadequate time for preparations, which included finding the sites and checking their facilities, dimensions, and licensing requirements.

There was also pressure from the Arts Council to play in middle-sized theatres in towns which already had an established theatrical life. Yet, despite the problems, the tour achieved its aim of presenting itself as the RSC and not as a 'second eleven' or a substitute for the 'real thing' left behind in Stratford or London. Lessons had been learnt, and, on the second 26-town, fifteen-week tour, from August to December 1979, the RSC took its own, flexible seating, which on average coped with between 400 and 470 people, as well as technical equipment and a stage, designed by Chris Dyer. This made the company independent of any of its venues. The tour was backed again by the Arts Council touring department and the private firm Hallmark Cards, which has a long history of supporting the arts and especially productions of Shakespeare on US television.

Now the guiding hand had moved from The Other Place to The Warehouse, which housed the administration team. Howard Davies was in charge of the tour and directed *Much Ado About Nothing*, his first Shakespeare for the RSC, while John Caird directed Brecht's *The Caucasian Chalk Circle*. Davies had wanted to take a third and new play — Barrie Keeffe's *Bastard Angel* — but this had to be dropped because of the economic cuts, though it was performed the following year at The Warehouse.

Research had shown that some of the venues would only take the RSC Shakespeare. They had to be persuaded that the Shakespeare was so good partly because of the RSC's belief in the benefits of cross-fertilization, and therefore they should see the Brecht as well. Others did not want to touch Shakespeare with a bargepole, and the argument had to be put the other way round. Two London boroughs cancelled performances because the shows did not include any star names — completely missing the point of the tour and of the RSC. Both shows went into The Warehouse in early 1980, while John Barton's production of *The Greeks,* the first RSC multi-play 'epic' since *The Romans*, played in the Aldwych.

Cross-fertilization with the 'main houses'

In 1980 the RSC faced the most serious crisis in its history, a crisis even more serious than the one that had been gathering ten years before. Looking back, 1970 did mark a turning point, dominated by Brook's *Dream*, which paradoxically said farewell to the 1960s while opening the next decade with its challenge to established RSC rehearsal and production practice. It was the year of Robin Phillips's modern-dress *Two Gentlemen of Verona* and Buzz Goodbody's disrespectful *King John*. It was also the year when the RSC pushed ensemble playing to extreme lengths, applying the notion mechanically by having leading actors appear as soldiers in *Hamlet* and leading actresses as monks in *Richard III*. At Stratford, the base of the RSC, two distinct approaches to Shakespeare had emerged — put crudely, the spectacular and the spartan. After *The Romans,* it seemed as if energy switched to the spare interrogations of The Other Place: these had a cohesion and direction lacking in the productions at the large Stratford theatre, which suffered a high cast turnover with fewer actors at the core than was healthy.

With the opening of The Warehouse, it seemed as if a further distinction were added. A new generation, defined by outlook and not exclusively by age, had come into the RSC with the egalitarian, social values of the fringe, and it was not committed primarily or necessarily to Shakespeare or to the belief in drama as a humanizing experience that made one a better person. This new situation hampered the cross-fertilization process: for example, director Terry Hands, who was made joint artistic director of the RSC in 1978, designer Farrah, and leading actor Alan Howard, all associated with one approach, had not worked in either of the small theatres by the time this book was written.

Also, those who represented the other strain worked uneasily in the larger Stratford theatre, with only Barry Kyle among the younger directors having mounted 'main stage' Shakespeare. When Nunn and a group of leading RSC actors and directors filmed two television shows (part of a commercial network's cultural series aimed at making the arts more popular), the subject was, simply, verse speaking — without any reference to cross-fertilization with modern writers, to the social context of the plays, or even to the Company's small-space discoveries. However, there was more exchange in design. The simplicity of the smaller spaces — which was not unknown to the larger theatres, for example in Christopher Morley's *Twelfth Night* in 1969 — did have its effect, from John Napier's wooden gallery set for the 1976 Stratford season, to Chris Dyer being appointed resident designer in 1978 in charge of both large theatres, to Morley's chamber set for *Caesar* in 1979. Ironically, some of the sets at the other spaces were simultaneously becoming more intricate, such as Koltai's design for *Baal*.

In London, the concentration on new writing at The Warehouse showed signs of siphoning off new playwrights from the Aldwych, the repertoire of which had understandably lost some bite after the death of Sir Peter Daubeny in 1975 and the end of his impressive World Theatre Seasons. The RSC had also had a bad time with new work at the Aldwych in late 1978, with the cancellation of Mike Leigh's new play and the poor reception of Steve Gooch's *Women Pirates* and David Mercer's *Cousin Vladimir*. The Company had been commissioning new writers since 1960 — Arden, Bolt, Shaffer, Whiting — urging them not to be constrained by size of cast or scale of theme; but apart from Peter Hall's commitment to Harold Pinter and David Jones's to David Mercer, living playwrights, let alone the radical generation of the 1970s, had received little consistent encouragement on the Aldwych stage. One problem after The Warehouse opened was that the knowledge, expertise, and contacts of its team were not properly fed into the Company as a whole. In a contradictory way, this reinforced the feeling of some writers that the RSC 'studio', like many others attached to 'main' theatres around the country, had become institutionalized, and that this helped keep its work off the big stages, away from large audiences. This also had to do with the changing role of the box office in a mixed economy, and the associated crisis for playwrights of representation, how to find the right 'form and content'.

The RSC in the 1980s

The problem remained of how to go forward in the worsening political and economic situation of the 1980s. Nunn had refused to be cowed by the Conservative Government's public spending cuts in 1979, or to make concessions to the philosophy that lay behind them. He continued to argue that the RSC worked better when it was doing ten things and getting eight right rather than trying to do two or three to perfection. But would he be able to hold this position? Critics in the right-wing press, and inside the Arts Council and the RSC, called for The Warehouse to be axed. Yet, ironically, the fact of its size, its existence on the margins of the Company's total budget, and its relative cost-effectiveness were defences against such attacks. The saving would be far too small to compensate for the artistic loss. Nunn also firmly stamped on the other idea of closing The Warehouse as a gesture, to show willingness to co-operate in the new economic climate. In one newspaper interview, he even went as far as to say, perhaps incautiously, that he would rather see the Aldwych shut.

There were also discussions about the size of the Company: should it be cut by half? This had always been an issue in the RSC — whether to have a large company, which would mean disgruntled spear carriers, or to have a small one in which everyone was overworked. But this time it was an economic and not an artistic debate. Schemes like the opening of the third Stratford auditorium had to be put off through lack of funds, and a US tour fell through at the last moment, though the RSC did sign a contract with a commercial television company, Thames, to have three shows filmed during the following three years. (Thames had already broadcast Nunn's production of *Macbeth*.)

A major headache for the RSC, which now grew more painful, was the planned move of its London base to the Barbican. A £1 million appeal to back the Company's work in the Barbican Centre for Arts and Conferences in the City of London had been launched on Shakespeare's birthday in 1978, but the response had been half-hearted. In any case, the move had been re-scheduled for 1980, then again to 1981, with a royal opening planned for 1982. The RSC's relationship with the Barbican had begun when the City engaged a leading theatre producer and friend of Hall's, who advised in 1964 the involvement in the scheme of a major theatre company and symphony orchestra. Their work would be linked to the Guildhall School of Music and Drama, which was having its own new premises in the Centre. This tied in with the RSC's constant desire to be involved in training, expressed in Saint-Denis's work and included in the Company's charter. The RSC also helped design the Barbican's 'one-room' wide theatre, seating up to 1,166 (larger than the Aldwych but smaller than the Stratford theatre), and the studio called The Pit, which is under the auditorium and has flexible seating for up to 200.

In March 1979 the topping out ceremony for the centre was performed by Sir Kenneth Cork, the Lord Mayor of the City of London and also the chairman of the RSC's governors. Some in the Company welcomed the delay in moving because they saw the transfer of the RSC's London operation to the multi-million-pound concrete complex as running counter to the aims and interests of the Company and likely to blunt any radical developments. After all, naming a seat for £500, which also let the nominee or sponsoring firm take part in an exclusive priority booking scheme, was hardly the way to reach new audiences. There were those who also felt that the Arts Council might like to offload the RSC onto the well-heeled City fathers. Despite a puritan streak, the RSC has never argued that self-denial makes for good artists, and the dangers of being bought off were very clear.

Nunn put his finger on the contradiction when he said: 'It is good for a company of our size to have a place in which to challenge itself and try different approaches. How else do we keep moving while remaining responsible to our paymasters and maintaining our standards?' There has to be a tension inside a company like the RSC between the new and the established, but when does it reach breaking point? Working at full stretch can be invigorating, but it can also leave you on thin ice. Until the end of the 1970s the tension was for the most part resolved creatively, with the system showing great flexibility in decision-making and in its ability to adapt to changed circumstances. But in 1980 could the RSC go on regenerating itself as it had done by skilfully using its own resources?

The return of a Conservative Government intent on putting the clock back coincided with a critical point in the RSC's history, and put either salvation or destruction on the agenda. It would be a hard economic battle, with all the difficulties of recouping revenue when the grant has been cut and with higher Value Added Tax hitting the theatre by pushing up the price of tickets, travel, and eating out. The success of the other spaces had sharpened the artistic crisis for the Company, which, like second Elizabethans conquering new territories with zeal and enterprise, had expanded to the point at which most 'extra-mural' activities had become part of the official programme, used for fund-raising, or were tried outside the Company in 'spare time'.

'Studio' was a dirty word for many in the RSC establishment when The Other Place opened. By 1980 it had become part of the establishment. Where would experiment next surface, and what form would it take? Like some of the characters in its own productions, the RSC had lost the space to stand back and judge. Maybe only a severe external crisis could shake it up, but would the outcome be the loss of an important national resource, not to mention its other spaces? If those spaces, having done a useful job, were saved, would they become part of a paralyzed theatre museum? Or would they, and the Company that created them, survive through the 1980s as a dynamic, rallying force?

86

Productions 1974-79
The Other Place

1974
10 Apr. *King Lear* (Shakespeare), dir. Buzz Goodbody, des. Anna Steiner
14 June *I Was Shakespeare's Double* (John Downie with Penny Gold), dir. Howard Davies, des. Martyn Bainbridge
27 Aug. *Babies Grow Old*, dir. Mike Leigh, des. Judith Bland
1 Oct.   *The Tempest* (Shakespeare), dir. Keith Hack, des. Maria Bjornson
3 Dec.   *Afore Night Come* (David Rudkin), dir. Ron Daniels, des. Andrea Montag
17 Dec. *Uncle Vanya* (Chekhov), dir. Nicol Williamson, des. Debbie Sharp

1975
8 Apr.   *Hamlet* (Shakespeare), dir. Buzz Goodbody, des. Chris Dyer
24 June *The Mouth Organ, or How To Prevent Lockjaw in Two Hours Ten Minutes* (Clifford Williams and Ralph Koltai), dir. Williams, des. Koltai
5 Aug.   *Perkin Warbeck* (Ford), dir. Barry Kyle and John Barton, des. Chris Dyer
22 Sept. *Man is Man* (Bertolt Brecht), dir. Howard Davies, des. Chris Dyer
7 Oct.   *Richard III* (Shakespeare), dir. Barry Kyle, des. John Napier

1976
31 Mar. *Schweyk in the Second World War* (Bertolt Brecht, transl. Sue Davies) dir. Howard Davies, des. Di Seymour
1 June   *Dingo* (Charles Wood), dir. Barry Kyle, des. Kit Surrey
4 Aug.   *Macbeth* (Shakespeare), dir. Trevor Nunn, des. John Napier
22 Sept. *Destiny* (David Edgar), dir. Ron Daniels, des. Di Seymour
3 Nov.   *Bingo* (Edward Bond), dir. Howard Davies, des. Chris Dyer

1977
19 May   *The Alchemist* (Ben Jonson), dir. Trevor Nunn, des. Chris Dyer
29 June *'Tis Pity She's a Whore* (John Ford), dir. Ron Daniels, des. Chris Dyer
4 July   *The Lorenzaccio Story* (Paul Thompson, after Alfred de Musset), dir. Ron Daniels, des. Chris Dyer and Jenny Beavan
7 Sept. *Queen Christina* (Pam Gems), dir. Penny Cherns, des. Di Seymour
2 Nov.   *Sons of Light* (David Rudkin), dir. Ron Daniels, des. Ralph Koltai

1978
24 Jan. *The Dance of Death* (Strindberg,), dir. John Caird, des. Mary Moore
3 May   *The Merchant of Venice*, dir. John Barton, des. Christopher Morley
21 June *Captain Swing* (Peter Whelan), dir. Bill Alexander, des. Kit Surrey
8 Aug.   *The Churchill Play* (Howard Brenton), dir. Barry Kyle, des. Kit Surrey
5 Oct.   *Piaf* (Pam Gems), dir. Howard Davies, des. Douglas Heap
27 Nov. *Hippolytus* (Euripides, realized by David Rudkin), dir. Ron Daniels, des. Ralph Koltai
18 Dec. *The Shepherd's Play*, dir. David Tucker, des. Pippy Bradshaw (local tour)

1979
28 Mar   *Pericles* (Shakespeare), dir. Ron Daniels, des. Kit Surrey
11 Apr. *The Jail Diary of Albie Sachs* (David Edgar), dir. H. Davies, des. Chris Dyer
6 June   *The Suicide* (Nikolai Erdman), dir. Ron Daniels, des. Kit Surrey
1 Aug.   *Baal* (Bertolt Brecht, transl. Peter Tegel), dir. David Jones, des. Ralph Koltai
18 Sept. *Anna Christie* (Eugene O'Neill), dir. Jonathan Lynne, des. Saul Radomsky
29 Sept. *Three Sisters* (Chekhov), dir. Trevor Nunn, des. John Napier

The Warehouse

1977-78

18 July   *Schweyk in the Second World War* (Bertolt Brecht, transl. Sue Davies), dir. Howard Davies, des. Di Seymour

20 July   *Macbeth* (Shakespeare), dir. Trevor Nunn, des. John Napier (also Young Vic)

26 July   *That Good Between Us* (Howard Barker), dir. Barry Kyle, des. William Dudley

1 Aug.   *Bandits* (C. P. Taylor), dir. Howard Davies, des. Andrea Montag

8 Aug.   *Bingo* (Edward Bond), dir. Howard Davies, des. Chris Dyer

1 Nov.   *Factory Birds* (James Robson), dir. Bill Alexander, des. Mary Moore

3 Dec.   *Frozen Assets* (Barrie Keeffe), dir. Barry Kyle, des. Sally Gardner

24 Jan.   *Dingo* (Charles Wood), dir. Barry Kyle, des. Kit Surrey

1978

10 Apr.   *The Lorenzaccio Story* (Paul Thompson, after Alfred de Musset), dir. Ron Daniels, des. Chris Dyer and Jenny Beavan

11 Apr.   *The Dance of Death* (Strindberg, transl. Michael Meyer), dir. John Caird, des. Mary Moore (also the Aldwych)

12 Apr.   *'Tis Pity She's a Whore* (John Ford), dir. Ron Daniels, des. Chris Dyer and Jenny Beavan

30 May   *The Sons of Light* (David Rudkin), dir. Ron Daniels, des. Ralph Koltai

13 June   *The Jail Diary of Albie Sachs* (David Edgar), dir. Howard Davies, des. Chris Dyer

3 July   *Savage Amusement* (Peter Flannery), dir. John Caird, des. Chris Dyer

25 July   *A & R* (Pete Atkin), dir. Walter Donohue, des. Douglas Heap

19 Sept.   *Shout Across the River* (Stephen Poliakoff), dir. Bill Alexander, des. Sue Plummer

2 Nov.   *Look Out . . . Here Comes Trouble* (Mary O'Malley), dir. John Caird, des. Sue Plummer

12 Dec.   *The Hang of the Gaol* (Howard Barker), dir. Bill Alexander, des. Chris Dyer

20 Dec.   *Awful Knawful* (Peter Flannery and Mick Ford), dir. John Caird and Howard Davies, des. Chris Dyer

1979-80

11 Apr.   *The Churchill Play* (Howard Brenton), dir. Barry Kyle, des. Kit Surrey

24 Apr.   *The Merchant of Venice* (Shakespeare), dir. John Barton, des. Christopher Morley

22 May   *The Innocent* (Tom McGrath), dir. Howard Davies, des. Chris Dyer

12 June   *Piaf* (Pam Gems), dir. Howard Davies, des. Douglas Heap (also the Aldwych, Wyndham's, and Piccadilly)

26 June   *Hippolytus* (Euripides, realized by David Rudkin), dir. Ron Daniels, des. Ralph Koltai

8 Aug.   *Sore Throats* (Howard Brenton), dir. Barry Kyle, des. Kit Surrey

20 Sept.   *Men's Beano* (Nigel Baldwin), dir. Bill Alexander, des. Kit Surrey

30 Oct.   *Captain Swing* (Peter Whelan), dir. Bill Alexander, des. Kit Surrey

18 Dec.   *Much Ado About Nothing* (Shakespeare), dir. Howard Davies, des. Chris Dyer (from small-scale tour)

21 Jan.   *Bastard Angel* (Barrie Keeffe), dir. Bill Alexander, des. Douglas Heap

28 Jan.   *The Caucasian Chalk Circle* (Bertolt Brecht, transl. James and Tania Stern with W. H. Auden), dir. John Caird, des. Chris Dyer (from small-scale tour)

26 Feb.   *The Loud Boy's Life* (Howard Barker), dir. Howard Davies, des. Douglas Heap